LET THE GOOD TIMES ROLL

5 Key Factors To Heaven On Earth

LET THE
GOOD
TIMES
ROLL

5 Key Factors To Heaven On Earth

MARK HANKINS

MARK HANKINS MINISTRIES
ALEXANDRIA, LOUISIANA

Unless otherwise indicated, all scriptural quotations are from the *King James Version* of the Bible.

Quotations of Smith Wigglesworth are taken from *Ever Increasing Faith*, Wayne E. Warner, ed., revised ed. (Springfield, MO: Gospel Publishing House, 1971).

Some quotations are the author's paraphrase.

Let The Good Times Roll:
5 Key Factors To Heaven On Earth

First Edition 2006

Published by
MHM Publications
P.O. Box 12863
Alexandria, LA 71315
ISBN 1-889981-13-3

Printed in the United States of America.

CONTENTS

Praying to the Father in accordance to the two prayers in Ephesians, and coming to Jesus in the renewed surrender of faith and obedience, he may receive such an inflow of the Holy Spirit as shall consciously lift him to a different level from the one on which he has hitherto lived.

- Andrew Murray

For this cause I bow my knees unto the Father of our Lord Jesus Christ, Of whom the whole family in heaven and earth is named, That he would grant you, according to the riches of his glory, to be strengthened with might by his Spirit in the inner man; That Christ may dwell in your hearts by faith; that ye, being rooted and grounded in love, May be able to comprehend with all saints what is the breadth, and length, and depth, and height; And to know the love of Christ, which passeth knowledge, that ye might be filled with all the fullness of God. Now unto him that is able to do exceeding abundantly above all that we ask or think, according to the power that worketh in us, Unto him be glory in the church by Christ Jesus throughout all ages, world without end. Amen.

Ephesians 3:14-21
King James Version

THE
HOLY SPIRIT
FACTOR

CHAPTER ONE: 1
CRANK THE CHAINSAW

There is a funny story about a country boy who cut trees for a living. You might call him a "redneck." He heard of a new piece of equipment that was supposed to make work a lot easier and faster called a chainsaw. He bought one from the store because the man said he could cut up to 30 trees a day with this new chainsaw. After using it for a few days, he took it back to the store and complained that he was only able to cut 2 or 3 trees a day. The store manager took the chainsaw from him and pulled the starter rope. With a loud noise, the chainsaw started. The country boy jumped back, startled by the noise, and said, "What is that?" Being as ignorant as he was, he had never cranked the engine!

Today many struggle in the work of the Lord because they have never been filled with the Holy Spirit. He is the power that enables us in every area of life. We must give the Holy Spirit His proper place everyday. My Dad always said, "The Holy Spirit is a genius. If you will listen to Him, He will make you look smart." If you ignore the Holy Spirit, you will not look very smart. Jesus said that you shall receive power after the Holy Spirit is come upon you. We thank God for the Holy Spirit. He is the Greater One who lives in us.

> ## WE MUST GIVE THE HOLY SPIRIT HIS PROPER PLACE EVERYDAY.

THE COMFORTER HAS COME

Before Jesus went to the cross and ascended to heaven, He spent much time teaching on the Holy Ghost in John 14 and 16. He said:

> *And I will pray the Father, and he shall give you another Comforter, that he may abide with you forever; even the Spirit of truth; whom the world cannot receive, because it seeth him not, neither knoweth him: but you know him; for he dwelleth with you, and shall be in you.*
>
> *- John 14:16, 17*

2

Nevertheless I tell you the truth; it is expedient for you that I go away: for if I go not away, the Comforter will not come unto you; but if I depart, I will send him unto you.

- John 16:7

The Amplified Bible gives these words to describe the work of the Comforter: Counselor, Helper, Intercessor, Advocate, Strengthener, and Standby. The ministry of the Holy Spirit is also described in John 16:7-15. Jesus was excited because He knew that the coming of the Holy Spirit would usher in a new day for believers.

The Holy Spirit will guide you into all truth and show you things to come. He will show, declare, and transmit the things of God the Father and the Lord Jesus Christ to you. Jesus said the Holy Spirit will move in you and dwell in you. He will bring

> ## THE HOLY SPIRIT TAKES EVERYTHING JESUS HAS DONE FOR YOU AND MAKES IT REAL TO YOU.

you into close fellowship with the Father and the Lord Jesus. The Holy Spirit takes everything Jesus has done for you and makes it real to you. He is the power and presence of the risen and triumphant Christ in you.

3

THE MIND OF A GENIUS

It is clear that the death, burial, resurrection, and the Word of God are very important. However, if that was all we needed, God would not have sent the Holy Spirit. The Holy Spirit is very necessary and it is essential that we know about Him. The reason we know the Holy Spirit is so important is because of how much time Jesus and the Apostle Paul spent instructing believers on the Him. We must recognize Him. We must respond and yield to Him. He is a Genius. He transmits the mind of Christ to us. We can think like God when we are filled with the Holy Spirit.

> IF YOU WANT TO STUDY THE MIND OF A GENIUS... BE FILLED WITH THE HOLY SPIRIT.

Spirit. If you want to study the mind of a genius, be filled with the Holy Spirit. He gives us uncommon intelligence, insight, and understanding.

WIN THE CASE

P.C. Nelson wrote the book of fundamental Bible Doctrines for the Assemblies of God denomination. He was a

Greek and Hebrew scholar, fluent in 32 different languages. He described the Comforter with the Greek word "Parakletos." He is our Advocate, Counselor, and Intercessor. When the Holy Spirit is working on our case we have a tremendous advantage. He has a reputation for winning cases.

The "Advocate/Counselor" is called in for His exceptional knowledge, expertise in protocol and procedure, and persuasive speaking ability. I'm glad we have the Holy Spirit helping us today.

UNCOMMON STRENGTH

William Barclay describes the work of the "Parakletos" this way:

The kind of comfort and consolation in distress which keeps a man on his feet, when, left to himself, he would collapse. It is the comfort which enables a man or woman to pass the breaking point and not to break. One who is called in to help in a situation with which a man by himself cannot cope. He exhorts men to high deeds and noble thoughts.

The prayer of the Apostle Paul in Ephesians 3:14-21 describes the kind of strength that the Holy Spirit supplies in the inner man of every believer. He strengthens us with mighty power, fills us with the fullness of God, and opens the supernatural for exceeding abundant blessing.

One of my heroes of faith, Smith Wigglesworth, wrote a book called, <u>Ever Increasing Faith</u>. Here are some of my favorite quotes on the Holy Spirit from that book:

I see everything as a failure except that which is done in the Spirit.

You can do more in one year if you are filled with the Holy Spirit than you can do in fifty years apart from Him.

It's impossible to over-estimate the importance of being filled with the Holy Spirit.

There is nothing impossible to a man that is filled with the Holy Spirit.

When you are filled with the Spirit, then you will know the voice of God.

The moment you are filled with the Holy Spirit persecution starts.

Anyone who is filled with the Holy Spirit might at any moment have any of the nine gifts of the Spirit in manifestation.

Being filled with the Holy Spirit is not a luxury, it is a commandment.

CHAPTER TWO: 2
THE
PARACLETE

The function of the Holy Spirit is to fill a man with a spirit of power and courage which would make him able triumphantly to cope with life. The narrowing of the word Comforter has resulted in the undue narrowing of our conception of the work of the Holy Spirit.

- William Barclay

STRENGTH FOR BATTLE

The word "Parakalein" was used in classic Greek to describe the verb form of "Parakletos". The Holy Spirit helps us to translate the death, burial, and resurrection of Christ into our personal victory. The Holy Spirit is not just consolation or sympathy in sorrow or distress, He does much more than that. William Barclay says it this way:

Someone who would exhort troops that are about to go into battle and face life threatening situations; rallying or cheering them to fight, to accept the risk of battle. It is the speeches of leaders and soldiers to urge others on; to put courage into the faint-hearted. One who makes a very ordinary person cope gallantly with a perilous and dangerous situation. It gives someone courage before battle and it exhorts men to noble deeds and high thoughts. Life is always calling us into battle and the One who makes us able to stand up to the opposing forces, to cope with and conquer in life, is the Holy Spirit.... He is the presence and power of the risen Christ.

The Holy Spirit is our Advocate. He is the Counselor for the defense. He is called in to speak in support of His character in order to enlist favor of the Judge. The Advocate will present someone else's case in the most favorable light.

The Holy Spirit never brings condemnation. He always reveals the blood of Christ. He is the lifting power of the church.

- Smith Wigglesworth

SEISMIC RETROFIT

The Holy Ghost never comes on you or works in you just to make you look good. He is actually strategically strengthening you in areas of your life so you can face any situation. When the storm is over and the dust clears, you will still be standing.

Years ago, I was driving through San Diego and noticed that some of the buildings had cables running from each of their corners to the ground. I had never seen that on a building before, so I wanted to know what it was. I found out that it was called seismic retrofit. They strategically strengthened these buildings so that when an earthquake hits, they will not collapse. These buildings are strengthened from corner to corner, inside and outside, so after the shaking of an earthquake, they will still stand.

I believe the Holy Ghost can give you some seismic retrofit. You may not have certain strengths in your life, but the

Holy Ghost will add things to you. He will strengthen you in your inner man. When the devil shakes you, you can say, "I'm still standing." Thank God for the Holy Spirit that is our Strengthener.

CHAPTER THREE: 3
BLUEBERRY
PANCAKES

Even the Spirit of truth; whom the world cannot receive, because it seeth him not, neither knoweth him: but ye know him; for he dwelleth with you, and shall be IN you.

- John 14:17

When Jesus spoke of the Holy Spirit, He said that He is not just coming to visit, but He is going to move and dwell in you permanently. That means the Holy Spirit is not just coming to visit, He is moving in. He is going to have a change of address. If you are going to visit someone, you only bring some of your stuff. If you are moving in, you bring ALL of your stuff.

ALL things that the Father hath are mine: therefore said I, that he shall take of mine, and shall show it unto you.

- John 16:15

12

EVERYTHING that the Father has is Mine. That is what I meant when I said that He [the Spirit] will take the things that are Mine and will reveal (declare, disclose, transmit) it to you.

- Amplified Bible

The Holy Spirit takes things that belong to the Father and Jesus, and transmits them to you. If you are filled with the Holy Spirit then you are filled with God. The Holy Spirit will expand you to make room for all He has for you.

When the Holy Spirit moves in, He is glad to be there. However, He

> **IF YOU ARE FILLED WITH THE HOLY SPIRIT THEN YOU ARE FILLED WITH GOD.**

needs room to bring all of His stuff. He can't get His stuff in until you get some of your stuff out. We are commanded to be filled with the Spirit.

And be not drunk with wine, wherein is excess; but be filled with the Spirit.

- Ephesians 5:18

I like this excerpt from Smith Wigglesworth's book <u>Ever Increasing Faith</u>:

> *The most important thing, the one thing that counts is to see that we're filled with the Holy Spirit, filled to overflowing. Anything less than this is displeasing to God. We are commanded by God to be filled with the Spirit, and in the measure you fail of this you are that far short of the plan of God. The Lord would have us moving on from faith to faith, from glory to glory, from fullness to overflowing. It is not good for us to be ever thinking in the past tense, but we should be moving on to the place where we dare believe God. He has declared that after the Holy Spirit is come upon us we shall have power. I believe there is an avalanche of power from God to be apprehended if we will but catch the vision. Paul wrote at one time, "I will now come to visions and revelations." God has put us in a place where He expects us to have His latest revelation, the revelation of that marvelous fact, CHRIST IN US, and what this really means. We*

can apprehend Christ fully only as we are filled and overflowing with the Spirit of God. Our only safeguard from dropping back into our natural mind from which we can never get anything, is to be filled and yet filled again with the Spirit of God and to be taken on to visions and revelations on a new line. The reason why I emphasize the importance of the fullness of the Holy Spirit is that I want to get you beyond all human plans and thoughts into the fullness of vision, into the full revelation of the Lord Jesus Christ. Do you want rest? It is in Jesus. Do you want to be saved from everything the devil is bringing up in these last times? Receive and continue in the fullness of the Holy Spirit, and He will be ever revealing to you that all you need for all times is in Christ Jesus your Lord.

COOKED IN THE BATTER

One of my favorite things to eat is blueberry pancakes. Trina doesn't fix them for me at the house because she knows I have enough trouble already with my weight. She gives me wheat toast instead. So if I go out to eat somewhere that serves blueberry pancakes I always ask the server, "Do these blueberry pancakes just have blueberries poured on them or are the blueberries cooked in them?" Once you have had blueberry pancakes with the blueberries cooked in them, you don't want to eat them any other way. When I eat blueberry pancakes I want the blueberries cooked in the batter. Every bite I take I want to hit a blueberry.

In the Old Testament, they just had blueberries (the Holy Spirit) on them. In the New Testament, the blueberries were cooked right in the batter. In other words, when you are filled with the Holy Spirit nothing in life can take a bite out of you without hitting a blueberry. When the devil takes a bite out of you, you can say, "Ha, ha, ha, devil, you just hit a blueberry! You just hit the Holy Ghost living on the inside of me!"

CHAPTER FOUR: 4
THE HOLY GHOST IS A GENIUS

The Holy Ghost is not just smart; He is a genius. When you listen, cooperate, and respond to Him He will make you look smart.

> *The Holy Ghost is a genius. If you will listen to Him, He will make you look smart.*
>
> *- B.B. Hankins*

When the enemy has a scheme or strategy to come against you or your family, the Holy Spirit will warn you. He's a genius. He knows what the devil has planned. The Holy Spirit also knows what God has planned for you. He is concerned with every area of your life. If you will listen to Him, He will make you successful.

Since He is a genius, He knows everything. He knows the mind of God and everything that Jesus has purchased for us. It is great to have a genius living in you. The Holy Ghost is also a gentleman and will not interrupt you. Until you stop and recognize Him, He will allow you to keep doing what you are doing.

> **THE HOLY GHOST IS A GENTLEMAN; HE WILL NOT INTERRUPT YOU.**

You must stop and say, "Alright, what would the Genius like to say?" I heard Kenneth E. Hagin (Dad Hagin), say the Lord told him, "If we would be led by the Holy Spirit He would make us rich." He said the word "rich" means to have an abundant supply. If we are led by the Holy Spirit, He will bring us into the blessing of the Lord and we will be a blessing to others. The Holy Spirit will help you in every area of your life. He will help you know who to marry, where to work, what kind of car to buy, when to buy a house, and what to do with your money. The Holy Ghost is a genius. He knows everything.

CHAPTER FIVE: 5
YIELD
TO THE
HOLY SPIRIT

Our only safeguard from dropping back into our natural mind where we can receive nothing from God is to be filled and filled again with the Holy Spirit.

- Smith Wigglesworth

My brother, Mike, pastors a great church in Rowlett, Texas, which is a suburb of Dallas. Recently, he was in a service where the Holy Spirit was moving. The Spirit of God began to move and the Holy Spirit manifested in great joy and freedom. The minister walked up to Mike and asked, "Why don't you yield to the Holy Spirit?"

My brother thought, "Yield, that's an interesting concept." He pulled out his Greek lexicon from his coat pocket to look up the word. In Greek, yield means "when a soldier presents himself to his commanding officer for orders." This word "yield" shows us how important it is for each of us to daily acknowledge, recognize, and respond to the Holy Spirit.

RECOGNIZE THE HOLY SPIRIT

Don't suppress the Spirit...

- 1 Thessalonians 5:19 – The Message Bible

Is it possible to suppress or resist the Holy Spirit? In Acts 7:51, Stephen spoke these words to the leaders of the synagogue, "...ye do always resist the Holy Spirit." If we are not sensitive to the Holy Spirit, we can override anything He wants to say. Ephesians 4:30 says, "And grieve not the Holy Spirit of God...." God will not violate our right to choose. We must learn to recognize the Holy Spirit and welcome Him into our lives daily.

> WE MUST LEARN TO RECOGNIZE THE HOLY SPIRIT AND WELCOME HIM INTO OUR LIVES DAILY.

RESPECT THE HOLY SPIRIT

The Holy Spirit is the Greater One that lives on the inside of us. Jesus said of the Holy Spirit in John 14:17, "...the Spirit of Truth...ye know him; for he dwelleth with you, and shall be in you." We need to reverence and respect the Holy Spirit in us and report to Him for orders.

RECEIVE THE HOLY SPIRIT

The Holy Spirit can do more in five minutes than you can do in five years.

- Smith Wigglesworth

There are so many things in this life that want to demand and command our time. Feelings are the voice of your body. Reason is the voice of your mind or soul. Your conscience is the voice of your spirit. The Holy Spirit will not force His way into your life.

THE HOLY SPIRIT WILL NOT FORCE HIS WAY INTO YOUR LIFE.

The Holy Spirit is a gentleman. He will only go where He is invited.

We must receive and make room for the Holy Spirit in our lives. Smith Wigglesworth also said:

No full gospel, Holy Ghost person should ever get out of bed in the morning without being filled with the Holy Spirit, getting lost in the Holy Spirit, and praying in the Holy Ghost.

RESPOND TO THE HOLY SPIRIT

Romans 8:14 says, "For as many as are led by the Spirit of God they are the sons of God." The Holy Spirit is not going to make us do anything. He just prompts us. It is then our decision to respond to Him. If we would listen and respond to the Holy Spirit, we could avoid trouble in every area of our lives because He knows everything. We must yield and not resist the Holy Spirit.

THE ANOINTING ABIDES IN YOU

But the anointing which ye have received of him abideth in you....

- 1 John 2:27

The Spirit of God lives in us. He is there to help us in every area of our lives. We must learn to recognize, respect, receive, and respond to the Holy Spirit. Instead of resisting the Holy Spirit, we must learn to yield to the anointing on the inside of us. The Holy Spirit will lead, instruct, and teach us as we recognize, respect, receive, and respond to Him.

CHAPTER SIX: 6
OUTPOURINGS
OF THE
SPIRIT OF GOD

In 1906, one of the greatest outpourings of the Holy Spirit occurred in California at Azusa Street. From this outpouring, revivals were sparked all over the world. In the article *History of the Azusa Street Revival* from the "Azusa Street Centennial," you will see a brief summary of the history and impact of the Azusa Street revival:

> *While great revivals were taking place around the world at the turn of the 20th century, perhaps the most noted outpouring prior to the Los Angeles revival occurred in January 1901 at the Bethel Bible School in Topeka, Kansas taught by Charles Parham. After studying the Bible and spending time in prayer, several students experienced the Baptism of the Holy Ghost and began to speak in other tongues. Agnes Ozman*

is reported to have been the first to receive the experience, followed by several other students and the teacher, Charles Fox Parham.

Meanwhile, William Seymour was traveling throughout the United States in search of a better life. An African-American from Louisiana, he was the son of former slaves. In 1905 Seymour traveled to Houston, Texas, in search of relatives. There he attended a black holiness congregation pastored by Lucy Farrow. Farrow moved to Kansas City to serve as a governess and cook for evangelist Charles Fox Parham, at which time Seymour became the interim pastor for the holiness congregation in Houston. In the late fall of 1905, Farrow returned to Houston and testified of her spiritual experience. She had been baptized with the Holy Ghost with the evidence of speaking in other tongues. Soon after Farrow returned to Houston, Parham relocated his ministry there as well.

Parham conducted services in Bryan Hall and taught training classes on many subjects including the Holy Spirit. Seymour was faithful in attending Parham's services and training sessions. However, due to segregation laws of the time Seymour was forced to sit in the hallway while listening to Parham and others teach. Nonetheless, Seymour hungered for more of God and was determined to learn.

In 1905, Los Angeles resident Neely Terry, who attended a small holiness church pastored by Julia Hutchins, made a trip to Houston, Texas. She attended the church that William Seymour was pastoring. Impressed by Seymour's character and messages on the Holy Spirit he received an invitation to minister at the church in Los Angeles.

Seymour arrived in Los Angeles on February 22, 1906 and began preaching two days later. On April 9, 1906, a breakthrough occurred as Edward Lee was baptized with the Holy Spirit and began to speak in tongues after Seymour had prayed with him. The two men made their way to the Asbery home. There they had a song, prayers and testimonies, followed by Seymour's sermon using Acts 2:4 as a text.

The crowds became too large for the Asbury home on Bonnie Brae Street and were moved to the yard. Soon this became too limited as well. The group then discovered an available building at 312 Azusa Street, which had originally been constructed as an African Methodist Episcopal Church. Thousands learned of the revival and were drawn to the meeting from all over the world.

On the platform, a black man [Seymour] sat behind two wooden boxes, one on top of the other. They were his pulpit.... Occasionally, as Pastor Seymour prayed, his head would be so low that it disappeared behind the top wooden box.... Many times waves of glory would come over the meeting room, and people would cry out prayers of thanks or praise as they received the baptism of the Holy Spirit.

This move of God was not only for Los Angeles, but it was for the whole world – even future generations. Ultimately hundreds of millions have been reached as an indirect result of Azusa Street.

27

It is time for us to experience the glory of God in our generation. Today, there are more than 600 million Spirit-filled, charismatic, pentecostal believers that are changing nations.

For this reason [seeing the greatness of this plan by which you are built together in Christ], I bow my knees before the Father of our Lord Jesus Christ, For Whom every family in heaven and on earth is named [that Father from Whom all fatherhood takes its title and derives its name]. May He grant you out of the rich treasury of His glory to be strengthened and reinforced with mighty power in the inner man by the [Holy] Spirit [Himself indwelling your innermost being and personality]. May Christ through your faith [actually] dwell (settle down, abide, make His permanent home) in your hearts! May you be rooted deep in love and founded securely on love, That you may have the power and be strong to apprehend and grasp with all the saints [God's devoted people, the experience of that love] what is the breadth and length and height and depth [of it]; [That you may really come] to know [practically, through experience for yourselves] the love of Christ, which far surpasses mere knowledge [without experience]; that you may be filled [through all your being] unto all the fullness of God [may have the richest measure of the divine Presence, and become a body wholly filled and flooded with God Himself]! Now to Him Who, by (in consequence of) the [action of His] power that is at work within us, is able to [carry out His purpose and] do super abundantly, far over and above all that we [dare] ask or think [infinitely beyond our highest prayers, desires, thoughts, hopes, or dreams]—To Him be glory in the church and in Christ Jesus throughout all generations forever and ever. Amen (so be it).

Ephesians 3:14-21
The Amplified Bible

THE
GLORY
FACTOR

CHAPTER SEVEN: 7
SPEAKING
OF HIS
GLORY

The voice of the Lord is upon the waters; the God of GLORY thunders... The voice of the Lord is powerful; the voice of the Lord is full of majesty. The voice of the Lord breaks the cedars... The voice of the Lord splits lightning... The voice of the Lord makes the wilderness tremble... The voice of the Lord makes the hinds bring forth their young, and His voice strips bare the forests, while in His temple everyone is saying, Glory!

- Psalm 29:3-9 - Amplified Bible

...in his temple doth every one speak of his glory.

- Psalm 29:9

God is called the "God of Glory" in Acts 7:2. In Ephesians 1:17, God is the "Father of Glory". In Psalm 24:7-10, He is the "King of Glory". In 1 Corinthians 2:8, Jesus is the "Lord of Glory". In Hebrews 2:10, we see that Jesus died to bring "many sons into glory". 2 Corinthians 3:18 says that we are changed from "glory to glory". 1 Peter 4:14 says, "...the Spirit of glory and of God resteth upon you." In 1 Corinthians 2:7, the Apostle Paul says of his revelation, "But we speak the wisdom of God in a mystery, even the hidden wisdom, which God ordained before the world unto our glory." Jesus is the Lord of Glory and came that we might enjoy the same glory (John 17:22-24).

THE GLORY...
CONTEND, CONTAIN, CARRY

Even the mystery which hath been hid from ages and from generations, but now is made manifest to his saints: To whom God would make known what is the riches of the GLORY of this mystery among the Gentiles; which is Christ in you, the hope of glory....

- Colossians 1:26, 27

God has called us in the new covenant to be carriers of the glory. We contain and carry the glory of Jesus. The glory of God is one of the most outstanding characteristics about God. It is literally His manifested presence. Even though God is everywhere, His presence is not manifested everywhere. At this time we must lift our voice and contend for the glory of God to be manifested in this generation. As we lift our voice and speak of His glory, there will be a radical change of scenery in our lives today.

> **THE GLORY OF GOD IS ONE OF THE MOST OUTSTANDING CHARACTERISTICS ABOUT GOD.**

> *Listen! I hear the voice of someone shouting, "Make a road for the Lord through the wilderness... The GLORY of the Lord will be seen by all mankind together." The Lord has spoken – it shall be. The voice says, "Shout!"*
>
> *Isaiah 40:3-6 – Living Bible*

The church of the Lord Jesus Christ is a glorious church. We carry the glory of the Lord in these last days. The prophet Habakkuk saw the vision of glory:

For the earth shall be filled with the knowledge of the glory of the Lord, as the waters cover the sea.

- Habakkuk 2:14

GLORY...GET LOADED

The Old Testament word for glory is "Kabod." It simply means "heavy." The best way to see it is "heavy" or "loaded" with the goodness of God. In 2 Chronicles 5 & 7, as the people praised God saying, "The Lord is good and his mercy endureth forever," the glory filled the temple. "Heavy" filled the house and the priests could not stand up. The manifested presence of God filled the temple. That is why today we can be so filled with the glory of God that we get "loaded" with God's goodness. We get saturated with the life of God.

RICHES IN GLORY...
TAP INTO THE TREASURY

One commentary I read defined the glory this way: wealth, numbers, commerce, power, wisdom, promotion, superiority, dignity, authority, nobility, splendor, valor, magnificence, extraordinary privileges, and advantages.

Whenever we say "GLORY," we are including all the goodness of God. We speak of His glory and carry His glory. This is why Satan hates us and tries to hinder us, but he cannot succeed because "Greater is He that is in you than he that is in the world," (1 John 4:4).

My God shall supply all of your need according to His riches in "Glory" by Jesus Christ (Philippians 4:19). Our prayers, faith, and giving tap into God's treasury... Glory! The New Testament word for glory is "Doxa." It is the light of the Gospel that shines and dispels all darkness and all the works of the devil.

CHAPTER EIGHT: 8
PREPARE FOR
GLORY
LIFT YOUR VOICE

Listen! I hear the voice of someone shouting, Make a road for the Lord through the wilderness; make him a straight, smooth road through the desert. Fill the valleys; level the hills; straighten out the crooked paths and smooth off the rough spots in the road. The GLORY of the Lord will be seen by all mankind together. The Lord has spoken - it shall be!

- Isaiah 40:3-5 - Living Bible

GENETIC CONNECTION

The voice of him that crieth in the wilderness, Prepare ye the way of the Lord... The GLORY of the Lord shall be revealed... Lift up thy voice with strength; lift if up, be not afraid; say unto the cities... Behold your God!

- Isaiah 40:3, 5, 9

Never underestimate the power of one voice. Never underestimate the power of a believer's voice. The voice of anyone who believes will literally move mountains and change the scenery.

A number of years ago I called my brother's church. The secretary mistook my voice for his voice because we're brothers and there is a genetic similarity. That's why families that sing

> WHENEVER WE SAY, "GLORY," WE ARE INCLUDING ALL THE GOODNESS OF GOD.

together have a special harmony. There is a genetic connection between the voices. Many times when I talk on the phone you can hardly tell the difference between my voice and my brother Mike's voice, or my voice and my son Aaron's voice. When I called Mike's church, they thought I was him and put me through to his secretary. She immediately said, "Pastor Mike." When she said that, I thought I would take advantage of the situation and said, "You know, I really love my brother Mark a lot and would like to express my appreciation to him in a more tangible way. I want you to send my brother Mark a check for $10,000." The secretary got real quiet on the other end of the phone because she thought I was Mike. Then I said, "I'm just kidding, this is Mark."

I realized my voice, because of the genetic connection, gave me access to his checking account. That's why God says, "Lift up your voice and speak." The genetic connection between you and Jesus Christ when you speak the Word of God causes angels to say, "That sounds like the voice of the Master to me." When you speak, there is an identical voice of faith; it sounds like the voice of God. When you lift up your voice, mountains have to move, sickness has to leave, and money has to come. There is authority, healing, deliverance, victory, and blessing in your voice.

> WHEN YOU SPEAK THERE IS AN IDENTICAL VOICE OF FAITH... IT SOUNDS LIKE THE VOICE OF GOD.

When you lift up your voice in faith and victory, angels are activated and it gives you access to the glory of God and the blessing of God.

BUILD A ROAD...
THE GLORY IS COMING

In Mark 11:23, Jesus said, "Whosoever shall say... he shall have whatsoever he saith." Anytime God wants to change someone's life, He always touches their mouth (Jeremiah 1:9, 10). Whenever God wants to change a nation, He will touch someone's mouth. He changes families, churches, and cities the same way.

Today, God is touching your mouth. God wants you to lift your voice as a believer moving mountains and preparing for the glory of the Lord. We must exercise our faith to prepare for the glory of God.

The move of God is voice activated. We must speak the Word of God. The spoken Word builds the road for the glory to come.

> **THE SPOKEN WORD BUILDS THE ROAD FOR THE GLORY TO COME .**

Your voice is your address in the realm of the spirit. As you lift up your voice, there is a sound that makes the way for God's will in our lives today.

Time is short – Jesus is coming soon! The glory of God will be seen in every nation. You are a carrier of the glory. Lift

43

up your voice! As the world gets darker and darker in these last days, the fire and the glory of God gets brighter and brighter in the church.

CHAPTER NINE: 9
EXPERIENCING
THEGLORY

Throughout the book of Ephesians, the Apostle Paul talks about experiencing the glory of God. The prayer in Ephesians 3 is a prayer for believers to pray that opens the supernatural. If you want to invite God to work in your life, this is a good prayer to pray.

I have always enjoyed going to an IMAX theater. These are great big theaters where the screen almost covers the entire room. One time I watched an IMAX film about two men that were climbing Mt. Everest. If you want to climb to the top of Mt. Everest, you are going to deal with a lot of strength issues. You will have to work out for a whole year before you even start and it will take you three months to get to the top. The reason it takes three months is because you have to stop at altitude camps on the way up the mountain.

At the first camp, you must stay for two weeks. Then you will go up to another altitude camp and stay there for a month. At each altitude camp, something happens to your blood. Actually, your red blood cells begin to increase because the oxygen is so thin at such high altitudes. By the time you reach the final altitude camp your blood has twice as many red blood cells as it did at the first altitude camp.

> THE GLORY IS NOT JUST SOMETHING THAT IS INTELLECTUAL; THE GLORY OF GOD IS SOMETHING THAT YOU EXPERIENCE.

What Paul is saying in Ephesians 3 is that God will strengthen your inner man. He will increase your capacity so you will be able to posses things in your life that are exceeding abundantly above what you could ever imagine. God wants to do something in you that will shock a generation.

Paul is speaking about being strengthened; this strength comes from His glory. What is the glory? The glory is not just something that is intellectual; it is something that you experience. Moses had a desire to see the glory. He cried out to God and said, "Show me your glory." David did the same thing in Psalm 63.

O God, thou art my God; early will I seek thee: my soul thirsteth for thee, my flesh longeth for thee in a dry and thirsty land, where no water is; To see thy power and thy GLORY, so as I have seen thee in the sanctuary.

- Psalm 63:1, 2

EXPERIENCE THE GLORY FOR YOURSELF

I remember when I was 17 years old, I cried out and said, "God, show me your glory. I can't live off my parents experience, I need to experience and see your glory for myself." You can't live off of another person's experience, sermon, or vision. You must experience the glory of God for yourself.

Paul said every believer should have an experience with the glory of God.

> YOU MUST EXPERIENCE THE GLORY OF GOD FOR YOURSELF.

Every believer should not only have an initial experience with the glory, but should go from glory to glory.

47

But we all, with open face beholding as in a glass the GLORY of the Lord, are changed into the same image from GLORY to GLORY, even as by the Spirit of the Lord.

- 2 Corinthians 3:18

> EVERY BELIEVER SHOULD NOT ONLY HAVE AN INITIAL EXPERIENCE WITH THE GLORY, BUT SHOULD GO FROM GLORY TO GLORY.

God wants you to experience more glory this year than you did last year. The man with an argument is always at the mercy of the man with an experience. When Paul stood before King Agrippa he explained his experience with the risen Christ. He said:

At midday, O king, I saw in the way a light from heaven, above the brightness of the sun, shining round about me and them which journeyed with me.

- Acts 26:13

Paul preached to the leaders of the Roman Empire and told them about his experience with the glory of the Lord Jesus Christ.

CHAPTER TEN: 10
THE GLORY: GOD'S
MANIFEST PRESENCE

Even though God is everywhere, He doesn't manifest His presence everywhere. He will only manifest His glory where He is invited; where somebody desires and believes in Him.

You must learn to let the Holy Spirit land on you. You will find out real quick the Holy Spirit doesn't land everywhere. If He hasn't landed on you in a while, you might want to find out what is wrong with your landing strip. When the Holy Ghost lands on you, the glory of God is manifested. When the glory of God is manifested, things begin to change.

> HE WILL ONLY MANIFEST HIS GLORY WHERE HE IS INVITED, WHERE SOMEBODY WANTS HIM AND BELIEVES IN HIM.

EXPOSED TO THE GLORY

The glory of God has the power to produce and birth things into your life that have never existed before. Look at Psalm 29:

> *The voice of the Lord maketh the HINDS TO CALVE, and discovereth the forests: and in his temple doth everyone speak of his GLORY.*
>
> *- Psalm 29:9*

> *The voice of the Lord makes the hinds bring forth their young...*
>
> *- Amplified Bible*

I have some friends in Louisiana that raise cows. Whenever they take a cow to the auction, they have to tell whether that cow has been "exposed" to a bull. When you get in the glory of God you will be able to say, "I've been exposed." When you get in the glory of God things are created. You will be able to conceive and new things will be born. God will put things in your spirit that nine months later you will give birth to. The reason the devil doesn't want you to get in the glory is because every time you come out you are carrying something from heaven that is going to be born in this earth. Things that didn't exist will come into being when they are conceived in the glory of God. The devil wants you to stay religious, but when you get hungry for the glory of God it will position you for something to be born in your life.

When I think of the wisdom and scope of his plan I fall down on my knees and pray to the Father of all the great family of God – some of them already in heaven and some down here on earth – that out of his glorious, unlimited resources he will give you the mighty inner strengthening of his Holy Spirit. And I pray that Christ will be more and more at home in your hearts, living within you as you trust in him. May your roots go down deep into the soil of God's marvelous love; and may you be able to feel and understand, as all God's children should, how long, how wide, how deep, and how high his love really is; and to experience this love for yourselves, though it is so great that you will never see the end of it or fully know or understand it. And so at last you will be filled up with God himself. Now glory be to God who by his mighty power at work within us is able to do far more than we would ever dare to ask or even dream of – infinitely beyond our highest prayers, desires, thoughts, or hopes. May he be given glory forever and ever through endless ages because of his master plan of salvation for the church through Jesus Christ.

Ephesians 3:14-21
The Living Bible

THE
FAITH
FACTOR

CHAPTER ELEVEN: 11
THE TRAJECTORY
OF FAITH

One day, I watched a championship golf match on television. One of the greatest golfers in the world stood on the green needing to make a very critical putt. Millions of people watched with millions of dollars at stake.

The golfer walked around on the green and viewed the location of the ball from several different angles. He carefully prepared to putt as the crowd watched almost breathlessly. When he hit the ball, it looked like he putted the wrong way! It looked as though he had misjudged the putt and the ball was off course.

Amazingly, the ball turned and headed right into the hole. As the crowd cheered, I sat there amazed that he had made the putt. I thought he had putted the ball the wrong way. However, from my view, I could not see the lay of the land on the green. The golfer actually had to putt the ball uphill because the direction and the pace of the ball were critical. He judged it perfectly and the ball landed right in the hole.

FAITH WILL GET YOU TO YOUR DESTINATION

As I thought about this, the Lord spoke to me, "I am a champion at 'putting' people in the right direction with the perfect pace so they can fulfill their destiny. When you think I am 'putting' you the wrong way, remember, I can see the lay of the land. I know your strengths and weaknesses. I will perfect that which concerns you," (Psalm 138:8).

> GOD IS A CHAMPION AT "PUTTING" PEOPLE IN THE RIGHT DIRECTION.

Every man or woman in Christ has a definite trajectory of faith and destiny. When it looks like God is "putting" you the wrong way, remember – He is a champion. He is able by His Spirit to get you in the right place at the right time to fulfill the call of God on your life.

FAITH GETS HAPPY NOW

When you look at the life of the Apostle Paul, you will see a man that God had perfectly "putt" to a divine calling and destiny. You can see the genius of God as you see the many turning points in the trajectory of Paul's life. You can also see the spirit of faith working to overcome adversity. Paul had been stoned, shipwrecked, snake-bit, beaten in the head, and left for dead. He could have said he was a tired, mistreated, lonely, disappointed, and hurting man. If you consider the adversity Paul encountered in his life, you would expect him to say something like that. Instead, Paul described himself as a happy man.

The joy of Jesus strengthened the Apostle Paul through all adversity. Paul's assignment was to assemble the thoughts given to him by Jesus and to publish the message throughout the body of Christ. God used him as a mouthpiece to speak and write to believers in every generation. In

> FAITH CRANKS GOD'S TRACTOR.

Philippians, one of his last letters, Paul speaks of joy and rejoicing sixteen times in four short chapters. Towards the end of his life, Paul stood before the leaders of the Roman Empire and said, "I think myself happy" (Acts 26:2). Another translation says, "I have been congratulating myself, King Agrippa."

> *...so that I might finish my course with joy...*
>
> *- Acts 20:24*

Paul's spirit of faith carried him to his divine destination. He finished his course with joy and completed the assignment given to him by Jesus Christ. He enjoyed the journey in spite of all the adversity he faced. Faith gets happy now!

THE KING STILL HAS ONE MORE MOVE

If you have ever been to Europe, especially France, you know that they have all kinds of art displays. I heard the story of a group that was touring the artwork at the Louvre. In that group was an international chess champion. The group was going through the Louvre looking at the artwork when they came to a picture that was titled, "Checkmate." The international chess champion was especially interested in this piece of artwork. The artist had drawn a chessboard where it looked like the king had no more moves. The picture showed the chess player with his head in his hands and the devil laughing at him. The group looked at the picture and moved on; but the chess champion stayed at the picture and stared at it. After a while, the leader of the group came back to check on him. The international chess champion said, "You know, they're either going to have to change the name of this picture or change the picture, because I am an expert and I can see that the king still has one more move."

This is also true of believers. Many of them have their heads down. The devil is laughing at them and it looks like it's all over. However, God wants you to know that you are going to have to change the name of the picture because the King has one more move! As you maintain a spirit of faith and let God make His move, the picture will reverse. Now the devil has his head down and you are the one that is laughing!

CHAPTER TWELVE: 12
FAITH
IS MOTION
ACTIVATED

I remember the first time I went into an airport bathroom where the water faucets were motion activated. I stood there looking for a handle or a pedal or something to turn on the water. I couldn't understand how this faucet worked. I saw this and thought, "We have a serious problem here; I don't know what their budget was, but someone has made a major mistake." It looked like the plumbing and the sink were there, but there were no handles. While I stood there trying to figure this out, a man walked into the restroom and waved his hand under the water faucet. Immediately, water began to come out. I stood there thinking I had just seen a miracle. I then saw people waving their hands under the hand towel dispenser and the towels would come out. That's when I looked up and saw a sign on the wall that said, "Equipment is motion activated."

In other words, God said, "Salvation is here, healing is here, deliverance is here and I am just waiting for someone to say 'I believe that' and to act in faith." While you are praising, rejoicing, and dancing around, the water begins to flow. Salvation, healing, and deliverance come – they are motion activated. One act of faith will open up the supernatural and cause the glory of God to come in. Jesus said in John 11:40, "...if thou wouldest believe, thou shouldest see the glory of God."

> **ONE ACT OF FAITH WILL OPEN UP THE SUPERNATURAL AND CAUSE THE GLORY OF GOD TO COME IN.**

> *...Didn't I tell you that if you believed, you would see the glory of God?*
>
> *- John 11:40 – The Message Bible*

BELIEVE IS A VERB

I recently watched a man on television who said that he had written the first novel that had no verbs in it. He said it was full of nouns, adjectives, pronouns, and prepositions, but no verbs. They asked him how well the book was selling and he said, "not very well." When asked why, he said, "because it has no action."

The word "believe" is a verb and verbs always denote action. Faith, on the other hand, is a noun. However, effective faith (faith that gets results) must be translated into action.

Even so faith, if it hath not works, is dead, being alone.

- James 2:17

So also faith, if it does not have works (deeds and actions of obedience to back it up), by itself is destitute of power (inoperative, dead).

- Amplified

For as the body without the spirit is dead, so faith without works is dead also.

- James 2:26

For as the human body apart from the spirit is lifeless, so faith apart from (its) works of obedience is also dead.

- Amplified

In my college psychology class, we learned that reasoning will not change an emotion, but action will. In other words, you can't feel your way into better behavior, but you can behave your way into better feelings. God created us where actions are stronger than feelings. Faith is an act. By faith we access the grace of God. Just a little bit of faith can access a whole lot of grace.

> REASONING WILL NOT CHANGE AN EMOTION, BUT ACTION WILL.

God has already done everything He is going to do about our salvation, our healing, our deliverance, and our blessing. Jesus paid it all and then sat down. Now it is our move – we have to know what He's done for us and act in faith on the Word of God.

Many churches are full of nouns, adjectives, pronouns, and prepositions but God is looking for verbs. He is looking for people who will believe and will act in faith. Faith moves God. faith moves mountains. Faith will not move anything until it moves you. The first part of you that your faith will move is your mouth.

Jesus said unto him, If thou canst believe, all things are possible to him that believeth.

- Mark 9:23

CHAPTER THIRTEEN: 13
FULFILLING YOUR DESTINY WITH A SPIRIT OF FAITH

I once watched a video documentary about salmon. The salmon is known as a fish with a fighting spirit. Noah Webster's 1828 dictionary defines and describes salmon this way, "A fish of the genus Salmon, found in all the northern climates of America, Europe, and Asia, ascending the rivers for spawning in spring, and penetrating to their head streams. It is a remarkably strong fish, and will even leap over considerable falls which lie in the way of its progress."

GOD'S GLOBAL POSITIONING SYSTEM

You may know the story of the salmon as they fight the current to go upstream to lay their eggs before they die. They challenge the strong current, rapids, rocks, and even bears, to reach their destination. Salmon have a remarkable Global Positioning System put in them by God that enables them to travel as much as 2,000 miles to locate the exact stream where they were born. They go up that particular stream, lay their eggs, and fertilize them. Their sense of direction, destiny, and determination is amazing.

The documentary said that there are bears in the streams trying to catch the salmon and end their journey. I found it interesting that the bears are actually after the salmon for their eggs because they like to eat the eggs more than the fish.

DIVINE ASSIGNMENT: THE EGGS YOU CARRY

The remarkable story of the salmon is similar to the life of faith and the fight of faith. The devil is not just trying to stop you; he is after the eggs you are carrying. God has an exact destiny for you. He has given every believer an assignment. When we finish the course God has designed for us and lay the eggs He has given us, our lives are

> THE DEVIL IS NOT JUST TRYIING TO STOP YOU; HE IS AFTER THE EGGS YOU ARE CARRYING.

multiplied a million times and reach into the next generation.

God is able to get you in the right place, at the right time with the right people. He has an exact destiny or stream that you should go up to lay your eggs. It takes a spirit of faith to locate this exact stream and overcome the adversity that comes against us as we do the will of God. This sounds similar to the Apostle Paul's life: "For a great door and effectual is opened unto me, and there are many adversaries," (1 Corinthians 16:9). God has a great effectual open door for your life. There is an open door for you but there are also many adversaries. In spite of the adversaries, you can walk through that door and do all of the will of God.

NEVER LOOK BACK IF YOU WANT THE POWER OF GOD IN YOUR LIFE.

Paul did the will of God and left some "eggs": New Testament letters (Romans, Corinthians, Galatians, Ephesians, Philippians, Colossians, etc.) that are still changing lives after 2000 years.

Keep believing and speaking and your faith will guide you into all God has for you. Your faith will open the door of the supernatural for you and many others to travel through. Smith Wigglesworth said, "Never look back if you want the power of God in your life." The spirit of faith goes forward and presses for those things that are ahead.

GOD'S OSCARS FOR ACTORS OF FAITH

The spirit of faith is necessary to do the will of God and finish the course He has for you. God wants you to finish your course, keep the faith, serve your generation according to the will of God, and finish with joy (2 Timothy 4:7, Acts 13:36).

The spirit of faith has an attitude and an action. Believing is the attitude and speaking is the action. When we keep our speaker connected to our believer, the spirit of faith carries us to our divine destiny.

Hebrews 11 lists some heroes of faith. The phrase "by faith" is used 20 times in reference to men and women who did the will of God. They received the promises of God in their generation and they are influencing the lives of millions of believers even today.

The Message Bible translates the phrase "by faith" as "by an act of faith." Faith is an act. Act like Jesus has done what He said he did. Act like you would if you already had the thing you are believing God for. Act like you are who He says you are. Act like you can do what God says you can do. Remember, faith is an act.

Hebrews 11 contains some of God's greatest actors. God gave OSCARS to these heroes of faith. Roll out the red carpet and get the camera ready! It is time for some more OSCARS and the awards are eternal!

CHAPTER FOURTEEN: 14

THE ATTITUDE OF FAITH

We having the same spirit of faith, according as it is written, I believed, and therefore have I spoken; we also believe, and therefore speak.

- 2 Corinthians 4:13

The spirit of faith affects every area of your life. Paul gives us two necessary ingredients to the spirit of faith – believing and speaking. Believing is the attitude of faith. You can choose fear and doubt, or you can have an attitude of faith.

I once read a book about a man named Viktor Frankl. Viktor was a Jew in a Nazi concentration camp in World War II. He lived in a flea infested and diseased area. He was constantly badgered, harassed, beaten, and made to carry burdens. Viktor said in this Nazi concentration camp, he could tell when a person

71

was getting ready to give up and die. He could look into people's eyes and see when their attitudes started to change. He could also see it in their posture as they walked, when hopelessness had taken over their life. Although physically they could have survived and lived longer, mentally they had broken down. Viktor said that he could tell when they were ready to lay down, stop eating, give up and die. He said he could see it in their attitude. Viktor Frankl determined that there was one thing the Nazis could

THE LAST OF ALL HUMAN FREEDOMS IS THE ABILITY TO CHOOSE ONE'S OWN ATTITUDE REGARDLESS OF CIRCUMSTANCES.

not control in his life; they could not control his attitude. He said, "The last of all human freedoms is the ability to choose one's own attitude regardless of circumstances." In other words, he couldn't control everything, but he could control himself and his attitude.

Even in the middle of adversity, your faith will get you to your destination. God will get you there if you will maintain a spirit of faith. You will have to speak to the mountains and master your attitudes. You may not be able to control what has happened to you in life, but you are able to control your attitude.

You have the choice to believe and speak what God says about you. You have the choice to be happy on the way to your divine destiny.

RISE UP IN FAITH

While ministering in Albuquerque, New Mexico, I went to a hot-air balloon festival. This event is the largest hot-air balloon festival in the world. It was an amazing sight with over 700 hot-air balloons flying in the sky at the same time. They had a competition to see which balloon could get closest to the designated target.

A man from the church I was ministering at actually had a hot-air balloon in the competition and took me in the balloon with him. Not long after we took off, he told me that we had absolutely no control over the direction of the hot-air balloon. He said the only thing that we had control over was the altitude of the balloon. We noticed that all of the balloons at 1,000 feet were headed south. The problem with that was the target was on the north side of Albuquerque. The man I was riding with pointed out that the balloons that had made it to 3,500 feet were heading north. There was a different wind blowing at 3,500 feet causing the balloons to go a different direction. So we climbed to 3,500 feet and gradually made our way down to the target. The only thing we could control was the altitude. By adjusting that, we made it to our destination.

MOVE UP HIGHER, ANOTHER WIND IS BLOWING

This experience reminds me of people following Jesus and obeying God. Many times you see everyone heading south and you think this is just the way life is. However, if you want to go a different direction and get on the target that God has for you, you are going to have to rise up in the Spirit, rise up in the reality of your redemption, and rise up in faith. If you are living by your feelings and circumstances you will be flying right at 1,000 feet and you will be headed south. If you will rise up in the spirit there is another wind blowing that will take you to the divine destiny God has for you.

CHAPTER FIFTEEN: 15

MOVE YOUR MOUTH
MOVE YOUR MOUNTAIN

Understanding how faith works is the essence of Jesus' words in Mark 11:23. It is interesting that Jesus' first phrase is "Whosoever shall say...." When we think of faith in God, we automatically think that faith is believing. As true as that is, Jesus begins His definition of faith with "say." Why does He start with "say" and end with "saith"?

The speaking part of faith is very important. Speaking must, in fact, be vital to faith working effectively. Jesus emphasizes the speaking part three times and believing only once. In Mark 11:23, we can see from Jesus' words that the speaking part must be emphasized 3 times more than the believing part. It must be true that faith moves mountains, but your faith must move your mouth before it will move your mountain.

CHANGE YOUR WORDS CHANGE YOUR WORLD

Faith moves God. Faith moves mountains. Faith will not move anything until it moves you. The first part of you that your faith will move is your mouth. Smith Wigglesworth said, "No man looks at appearances if he believes God. I'm not moved by what I see, I'm not moved by what I feel, I'm moved only by what I believe, and I believe God." I am moved by what I believe! Believing must move your mouth first. Your faith must move your mouth to move your mountain. Your faith must change your words before it will change your world. If you are silent, you lose by default. There is no silent faith in the Bible. Faith must have a voice.

LIVING FAITH WILL CARRY YOU

Faith without works is dead (James 1:17). One translation says, "Faith without corresponding actions is dead." Faith is an act. Faith without action is dead. It is so difficult to carry dead faith around; however, living faith will carry you. Living faith demands action.

The first act of faith is to move your mouth. There are other acts of faith, but moving your mouth is essential to faith. Romans 10:8-9 says, "What saith it? The word is near you, in your mouth and in your heart, that is the word of faith which we preach. That if thou shalt confess with thy mouth the Lord Jesus and shalt believe in thine heart God raised Him from the dead, thou shalt be saved." Again, the word of faith begins in your mouth.

The first act of faith a Christian makes is with his mouth saying, "Jesus is Lord." The miracle of the new birth is activated by words. There are many important facets of faith, but the speaking part is vital. It seems that Satan wants to stop you before

> **YOUR FAITH MUST CHANGE YOUR WORDS BEFORE IT WILL CHANGE YOUR WORLD. IF YOU ARE SILENT, YOU LOSE BY DEFAULT.**

the initial act of faith. When God gets his foot in the door, His power changes everything.

SATAN CANNOT MAKE A CHAIN THAT FAITH IN GOD CANNOT BREAK

Now we can see the importance of understanding faith. Let us also understand that we open the door to the supernatural through speaking and believing. However, we still cannot figure out with our finite intelligence how God is working our miracle. We are the believer - GOD IS THE PERFORMER! We don't have to make it all happen. We just activate our faith and God brings the miracle to pass however He chooses. We are not replacing God, WE ARE RELEASING GOD!

By faith, we can enter into rest and let God do His part. Our part is to speak and to believe and God's part is to do what we could never do on our own. Have faith in God. God is pleased by faith. He is looking for faith. He has given us His Word to feed our faith. He has given us clear instructions on how faith works. We have the same spirit of faith. Smith Wigglesworth said, "Any man can be changed by faith, no matter how he may be fettered." Satan cannot make a chain that faith cannot break. Jesus breaks every chain and sets us free.

FAITH IN GOD CAN CHANGE ANYTHING

I have a niece that used to live in Italy. One day she came home with her paper from grade school and was crying. She had drawn a picture and one of the kids from the class had taken her paper and put a big ugly mark on it. She is a tenderhearted girl so she was very upset. Her mom, trying to comfort her, encouraged her to settle down. She then took a pen and began to try to fix the picture. She started working with the ugly mark and before long, it had become a beautiful flower.

Many people spend their lives whining and crying about what the problems of life have done or what kind of mark the devil has put in their life. If we will go to God and let Him show us a new picture, He will take the marks and turn them into something beautiful.

When you have a spirit of faith, you don't just see the problems and the bad experiences you have had, you see what God can do when you come to Him. You can boldly say, "I have a spirit of faith. It may look like something bad has happened to me, but I believe that God is going to make something good out of it." God never has said, Uh Oh! Faith in God can turn any situation around.

CHAPTER SIXTEEN: 16
ALL IS FORGIVEN

I, even I, am he that blotteth out thy transgressions for mine own sake, and will not remember thy sins. Put me in remembrance: let us plead together: declare thou, that thou mayest be justified.

- Isaiah 43:25-26

In Earnest Hemingway's short story, [1]*The Capital of the World,* he tells the story about a father and his teenage son who lived in Spain. Their relationship became strained, eventually shattered, until the son ran away from home. The father began a long journey in search of his lost and rebellious son. Finally, as a last resort he put an ad in the Madrid newspaper. His son's name was Paco, a very common name in Spain. The ad simply read, "Dear Paco, meet me in front of the Madrid newspaper office tomorrow at noon. All is forgiven. I love you." The next day at noon, in front of the newspaper office, there were 800 "Pacos" all seeking forgiveness.

COME HOME...BE BLESSED

I have blotted out, as a thick cloud, thy
transgressions, and, as a cloud, thy sins:
return unto me; for I have redeemed thee.

- Isaiah 44:22

God is in the forgiveness business. Today many people have trouble accepting the fact that God offers total forgiveness. Psalms 32:1 says, "Blessed is he whose transgression is forgiven, whose sin is covered." The Apostle Paul refers to this verse in

GOD IS IN THE FORGIVENESS BUSINESS.

Romans 4:6-8. This forgiveness includes the total erasing from His memory that sin was ever committed. He does this for His own sake so He can bless us the way He wants.

When we believe we are forgiven by God Himself, He

can bless us as only He can. If God doesn't remember that we have done anything wrong, then we should allow Him to erase it from our memory also. Smith Wigglesworth said, "Never look back if you want the power of God in your life." God's power is always propelling us forward.

NO MORE PARALYSIS

The story of the man with four crazy friends in Luke 5:17-26 is one of my favorites. "When Jesus saw their faith," He told the man with paralysis, "Man, thy sins are forgiven thee." Jesus spoke to that man's deepest need. If Jesus calls you forgiven, you are totally forgiven and released from the condition and consequences of sin. You are redeemed.

Jesus then told the paralyzed man to "Arise!" The man got up totally healed of all paralysis. This miracle caused the religious leaders much trouble. The rules and regulations of religion have paralyzed many people. However, when you get in the presence of Jesus, forgiveness and restoration are freely given. What a wonderful Jesus we have who forgives and heals! He is our Redeemer today.

REMIND ME OF THIS PROMISE

In Isaiah 43:25-26, we know God's promise says that He blots out our transgressions and will not remember our sins. However, we are to put God in remembrance of His Word. God says remind me of this promise. This promise of forgiveness and faith in His Word opens the door to God's goodness.

I once heard Dad Hagin say, "Faith will not work in an atmosphere of unforgiveness. If the devil can get you in condemnation – he'll cheat you out of your inheritance." When we receive forgiveness and freely forgive ourselves and others, our faith will work properly. God forgives us so radically and totally, that He commands us to forgive others the same way. God's kind of forgiveness erases the memory of all sin, failure, guilt, and accusation. We plead our case with the Word of God and the blood of Jesus.

Who forgiveth all thine iniquities; and who healeth all thy diseases.

- Psalms 103:3

Who shall lay anything to charge of God's elect? It is God that justifieth. Who is he that

*condemneth? **It is Christ that died, yea rather,
that is risen again, who is even at the right hand
of God, who also maketh intercession for us.***

- Romans 8:33-34

In 2 Corinthians 5:21, God declares us righteous in Christ. Righteousness is a free gift and those that receive it will reign in life through Christ Jesus (Romans 5:17). This revelation of righteousness makes us glad. These are days of Heaven on Earth, so go ahead and laugh at the devil. This is the day the Lord has made, so rejoice and be glad! Dare to declare that you are righteous in Christ!

[1]*Be A People Person*, John Maxwell

When I think of the greatness of this great plan I fall on my knees before the Father (from whom all fatherhood, earthly of heavenly, derives its name), and I pray that out of the glorious richness of his resources he will enable you to know the strength of the Spirit's inner re-inforcement—that Christ may actually live in your hearts by your faith. And I pray that you, firmly fixed in love yourselves, may be able to grasp (with all Christians) how wide and deep and long and high is the love of Christ—and to know for yourselves that love so far beyond our comprehension. May you be filled through all your being with God himself!

Now to him who by his power within us is able to do infinitely more than we ever dare to ask or imagine—to him be glory in the Church and in Christ Jesus for ever and ever, amen!

Ephesians 3:14-21

Phillips

THE
JOY
FACTOR

CHAPTER SEVENTEEN: 17

I BROUGHT YOU
HERE TO HAVE
A GOOD TIME

Several years ago, Trina and I took our children to Disney World in Florida. It was such a creative and exciting place for children with a lot of rides and entertainment. It was also quite an expensive trip for our family. I thought it was funny when I saw a mother scolding and correcting her little boy. The little boy had been whining, grouchy, and complaining. The mother grabbed him firmly by the arm and said, "I brought you here to have a good time, and you're going to have a good time!" The mother commanded him to stop complaining and whining, and to get happy right away. She went on to explain to the boy why he was commanded to have fun. She said, "I paid too much for this trip for you to be grouchy and complaining. It has taken us too long to get here for you to ruin it with your whining!" The little boy promptly dried his tears, stopped whining, and enjoyed the rest of the trip. I laughed because I understood exactly how that mother felt.

I Brought You Here To Have A Good Time

ENJOYING THE TRIP

Now I can imagine our Father God having a similar problem with some of his children. I can hear Him saying:

I brought you here to have a good time – now you are going to have a good time! I paid too much for your freedom for you to be bound - I paid too much for your joy for you to be depressed - I paid too much for your peace for you to be confused - I paid too much for your forgiveness for you to be condemned - I paid too much for your righteousness for you to be guilty or ashamed - I paid too much for your healing for you to stay sick - I paid too much for your success for you to fail!

The price of our freedom was the precious blood of Jesus. Jesus paid too high a price for our blessing for us to be cursed. We are blessed in Christ. God is speaking to us saying, "I brought you here to have fun - NOW YOU ARE GOING TO HAVE FUN!!!" It is time to enjoy our victory in Christ! It is time to enjoy our redemption!

91

EXCEEDING JOY USHERS
IN THE GLORY OF GOD

...yet believing, ye rejoice with joy unspeakable and full of glory.

- I Peter 1:8

...you believe in Him and exult and thrill with inexpressible and glorious (triumphant, heavenly) joy.

- Amplified Bible

Faith is activated by rejoicing. Believing is always accompanied by joy. In 1 Peter 1:8, the Apostle Peter speaks of some kind of wild, ecstatic, triumphant, heavenly joy...not some day when we get to heaven, but right now. Unspeakable joy is a container of the glory of God. The glory

BELIEVING IS ALWAYS ACCOMPANIED BY JOY.

and the abundance of God are manifested in an atmosphere of rejoicing.

God brought us here to have fun - now we are going to have fun! God brought us here to have victory - now we are going to have victory. We are commanded to rejoice; it is not an option.

This is the day which the Lord hath made; we will rejoice and be glad in it.

- Psalm 118:24

Rejoice in the Lord alway and again I say, Rejoice.

- Philippians 4:4

...the joy of the Lord is your strength.

- Nehemiah 8:10

EXCESSIVE CELEBRATION

Therefore with joy shall ye draw water out of the wells of salvation.

- Isaiah 12:3

You can make a withdrawal from your salvation account with joy. The wells of salvation are reservoirs of healing and blessing. Joy is your bucket to draw out your blessing. If you have great joy, you have a great bucket to draw much salvation.

My brethren, count it all joy when you fall into divers temptations...

- James 1:2

93

He did not say that it was a "joy" to have multiple troubles. He said to "count" it joy. Look at your problems and count. One joy...two joy...three joy...then laugh at the devil! What Satan meant for evil, God is turning around for your good. God paid too high a price for your victory for you to be defeated. Ha! Ha! Ha!

One translation of James 1:2 says to count it "Maximum Joy." I like that! Smile, laugh, jump, shout, then dance - turn it up and things will turn around. Joy unspeakable is full of glory. The glory of God is in joy. There is no penalty for excessive celebration in the kingdom

THERE IS NO PENALTY FOR EXCESSIVE CELEBRATION IN THE KINGDOM OF GOD.

of God. God brought you here to have dominion - now you are going to have dominion! God brought you here to have a good time - now you are going to have a good time!!!

94

CHAPTER EIGHTEEN: 18
YOU'VE GOT TEN SECONDS
TO GET ENTHUSIASTIC

I have a friend who is a very wealthy businessman. He loves Jesus very much and attributes his success to his faith in God. He has a sign in his office that says, "You have 10 seconds to get enthusiastic or get out of my office." I am sure this sign helps inspire friends and employees.

As he told me the story of how he likes to be around people that are enthusiastic, I imagined that God has a sign like this in His office. When you come into the Holy of Holies, God expects you to act like He is the Almighty God. He is the God of Glory and the Father of our Lord Jesus Christ. There is no one like Him. He alone is omniscient (all-knowing) and omnipotent (all-powerful). In His presence is fullness of joy. You have 10 seconds to get thrilled with who He is and what He has done for you in Christ or get out of the office!

Noah Webster, in his 1828 <u>American Dictionary</u> <u>of the English Language</u> defines enthusiasm as:

1. To infuse a divine spirit

2. A belief that one has special divine communications from the Supreme being, or familiar intercourse with Him.

3. Heat of imagination; violent passion or excitement of the mind, in pursuit of some object, inspiring extravagant hope and confidence of success.

CHRIST IN GOD...CHRIST IN YOU... YOU IN CHRIST

That he would grant you, according to the riches of his glory to be strengthened with might by his Spirit in the inner man.

- Ephesians 3:16

May He grant you out of the rich treasury of His glory to be strengthened and reinforced with mighty power in the inner man by the

[Holy] Spirit [Himself indwelling your innermost being and personality].

- Amplified Bible

We are infused with inner strength by the Spirit of God. As we invite God to fill us and strengthen us, something begins to happen in our spirit. There is a new enthusiasm about life and the will of God for our lives. As we recognize and yield to the Holy Spirit, God is able to do exceeding abundantly above all we can ask or think. We have "joy unspeakable and full of glory," 1 Peter 1:8.

What a great day we live in because of what Jesus has done for us. We are redeemed because of His death, burial, resurrection, and the power of His blood. The Spirit of God lives in us! Jesus explains this day of redemption in John 14:16-20. Notice verse 20 in the Amplified Bible:

At that time [when that day comes] you will know [for yourselves] that I am in My Father, and you [are] in Me, and I [am] in you.

What a powerful revelation given by the Holy Spirit. You are in Christ, Christ is in God, and Christ is in you! When we are filled with the Holy Spirit and yield to Him, He makes our redemption real to us. "This is the day the Lord has made, let us rejoice and be glad in it," Psalm 118:24. You've got 10 seconds to get excited about that and act like the greater One is in you now!

CHAPTER NINETEEN: 19

JOY: THE BRIDGE BETWEEN
BELIEVING AND RECEIVING

---

*Whom having not seen, ye love; in whom,
though now ye see him not, yet believing, ye
rejoice with joy unspeakable and full of glory:
Receiving the end of your faith...*

- I Peter 1:8,9

Faith has a beginning and faith has an end. Joy unspeakable and full of glory is the bridge between believing and receiving. Psalm 2 says that in the midst of adversity, God sits in the heavens and laughs. The Bible says the Kingdom of God is righteousness, peace, and joy in the Holy Ghost (Romans 14:17). The Kingdom of God is the realm of God; the place where God rules and reigns. If you want the Kingdom of God to break loose in your life, then joy is the supernatural battle strategy. Get full of joy and the dominion of God will breakout. Healing and blessing will break out. You cannot have joy and be unhappy. One thing about it, I don't think the devil can hang around happy people. The faster you get happy, the faster the devil is out!

> *... you believe in Him and exult and thrill with inexpressible and glorious (triumphant, heavenly) joy. [At the same time] you receive the result (outcome, consummation) of your faith...*
>
> *- 1 Peter 1:8, 9 - Amplified*

LAUGHING AT IMPOSSIBILITIES

> *And Sarah said, God hath made me to laugh, so that all that hear will laugh with me.*
>
> *- Genesis 21:6*

In Genesis 21, we find the story of Abraham and Sarah receiving a promise from God. They were old and well-stricken in age but God promised them a son in order to establish His eternal covenant. God told Abraham that He was going to bless Sarah. He said, "I will bless her, and she shall be a mother of nations; kings of people shall be of her," Genesis 17:16.

Through faith also Sarah herself received strength to conceive seed, and was delivered of a child when she was past age, because she judged him faithful who had promised.

- Hebrews 11:11

How did Sarah receive strength to conceive? She laughed and received strength for her miracle. She judged Him faithful that promised. She knew that what God had promised He was able to perform. Through faith she received strength. She said "God made me laugh."

The only thing most people think about is the conception. In

FAITH LAUGHS AT IMPOSSIBILITIES.

other words, they can only think about the baby or the miracle. The Holy Ghost is not just interested in the miracle, He's interested in you receiving strength. When the Word hits your spirit, there can be conception and you can give birth to your miracle.

Smith Wigglesworth said, "Faith laughs at impossibilities." Sarah first laughed in unbelief, but at some point she must have started laughing in faith. She must have said, "I'm not the performer; I'm just the believer." Sarah and Abraham then named their miracle "ha, ha." They named him Isaac, which means "laughter."

SUPERNATURAL JOY

Happy is the people that know well the shout of praise, that lives, Lord, in the smile of thy protection!

- Psalm 89:15 - Knox

The people that know the joyful sound are the ones who get into the presence of God and walk in the light of His countenance. This joy is not dependent on how much money you have in the bank or who likes you; it is supernatural. It comes from heaven. It comes from God. God has this joy in Him and as believers, the same joy is in us.

So how do you demonstrate this supernatural joy? You demonstrate it by rejoicing, smiling, and laughing. I believe joy irritates the devil. He hangs out in places of depression, grief, and sorrow. But where there is joy, the presence and glory of God will come in and run the devil off!

RECEIVING THE END OF YOUR FAITH

The bridge from believing to receiving is joy unspeakable. Many people never receive their miracle because they never get happy enough to believe "I have it right now; it's mine." 1Peter 1:9 says, "Receiving the end of your faith...." One translation says, "the outcome of your faith."

Your faith has a beginning, a middle, and an end. In the middle of a faith fight, you have to tell the devil how it is going to turn out. Jesus is the Author and Finisher of your faith. Your situation may look bad right now, but everything is going to turn out alright!

BELIEVING AND REJOICING

And blessed is she that believed: for there shall be a performance of those things which were told her from the Lord.

- Luke 1:45

You are not the performer; you are just the believer. There is no pressure on you whatsoever to perform that thing that God has spoken to you. You do not have to try to make it happen. The only pressure on you is to keep the switch of faith turned on. You do that by believing, speaking, and acting like the Bible is true. Rejoice that what God has promised, He is also able to perform. When you begin rejoicing, laughing, and shouting by faith, something happens in the spirit realm and the glory finds a place to land!

CHAPTER TWENTY: 20
SACRIFICES OF JOY

For in the time of trouble, He shall hide me in His pavilion: in the secret of His tabernacle shall He hide me; He shall set me up upon a rock. And now shall mine head be lifted up above mine enemies round about me: therefore, will I offer in His tabernacle sacrifices of joy; I will sing, yea, I will sing praises unto the Lord.

- Psalm 27:5,6

David said, "I get in the presence of God and I offer Him sacrifices of joy." What would that look like? In other translations it says, "sacrifices of shouting." Can you imagine David getting in the presence of God?

I remember one time as I was leaving my place of prayer,

the Holy Ghost said, "You're not going to dance? The Father likes it when you dance." So here I am trying to be spiritual and dignified, and God wants me to dance. I began to dance and say, "Hallelujah, hallelujah, can't nobody do me like Jesus, ha, ha, ha!" Suddenly, the Holy Ghost came on me. I thought, "He does like that! I believe I will do that again!" I found out that one of the greatest things it did was crucify my flesh because my flesh did not want to act like that.

FAITH AIN'T PRETTY

I saw an advertisement on television that the Lord used to talk to me about faith. It went something like this:

Hello neighbor! Tires ain't pretty, but everybody needs tires. So you might as well get your tires from me at discount tires.

A few weeks after I saw this advertisement, I was at church and the Spirit of God began to move in the service. People began to respond to the Holy Spirit. They were jumping, running, dancing, laughing, and just acting ridiculous. The Holy Ghost said to me:

Hello neighbor! Faith ain't pretty, but everybody needs faith. So you might as well release your faith right now.

Those people were not ashamed to get ugly for Jesus! If you are really concerned about looking pretty, it's going to make it difficult to be effective in the realm of the spirit. God doesn't want everyone to look pretty when they get around Him; He just wants them to get wild! Smile, jump, run, laugh, dance, and shout! God brought you here to have dominion. There is no penalty for excessive celebration in the kingdom of God. God has chosen the foolish things of this world to confound the mighty.

REJOICING: A FORM OF HUMILITY

In 2 Samuel 6, the Ark of the Covenant was coming into Jerusalem. The Bible says when the ark came into the city, King David danced before the Lord with all of his might. The scripture says he threw off his royal robe and danced in his under clothes because of the glory that was coming back! David loved to be in the presence of God!

After he danced before the Lord, David fed the entire nation. When he went to bless his household, his wife told him that he looked like a fool. She despised him in her heart because of his response to the presence of God. She thought he should have been more dignified. David responded to her by saying, "I should be more vile than this. I will humble myself in the sight of the people and I will lower myself in my own sight," verse 22.

> *...God resisteth the proud, but giveth grace unto the humble.*
>
> *- James 4:6*

When David was rejoicing, it was a form of humility. If you are more concerned with what people think about you than what God thinks about you, you will never walk in victory. Humble yourself in the sight of the Lord and He will lift you up!

CHAPTER TWENTY ONE: 21
THE SECRET POWER OF JOY

But let the righteous be glad; let them rejoice before God: yea, let them exceedingly rejoice.

- Psalm 68:3

...be in high spirits and glory before Him!
...glory before God, yes, let them [jubilantly] rejoice!

- Amplified

...Oh, Rejoice in His presence.

- Psalms 68:4 - Living Bible

...therefore will I offer in his tabernacle sacrifices of joy...

- Psalm 27:6

...sacrifices of triumphant joy...

- Rotherham

Because thou hast been my help, therefore in the shadow of thy wings will I rejoice.

- Psalm 63:7

That you are my help and in the shadow of your wings I shout for joy.

- NAB

THE WIGGLESWORTH SHUFFLE

In Dr. Lester Sumrall's book entitled <u>Pioneers of Faith</u>, He gave this account of one of his personal visits with Smith Wigglesworth:

> *One day, I asked Him, "Brother Wigglesworth, how is it that you look the same every time I come? How do you feel?" He bellowed at me like a bull and said, "I don't ever ask Smith Wigglesworth how he feels!" I asked, "How do you get up in the morning?" He said, "I jump*

out of bed! I dance before the Lord for at least ten to twelve minutes - high-speed dancing. I jump up and down and run around my room telling God how great He is, how glad I am to be associated with Him and to be His child." After this, he would take a cold shower, read the Bible for an hour, then open his mail to see what God would have him do that day. He was an extremely remarkable man, totally sold out to God.

Wigglesworth was known as a man of great faith and power. Maybe it seems unusual for a man like that to get up in the morning and dance, jump, and rejoice before God, but the supernatural signs and miracles that happened in his life were outstanding. Yet as we study the Bible, we see some excessive rejoicing by David, Job, Sarah, Mary, Elizabeth, Peter, and the Apostle Paul.

Rejoice in the Lord alway: and again I say, Rejoice.

- Philippians 4:4

WHAT HAPPENS WHEN YOU REJOICE

One day, the Lord spoke to me so clearly and said, "If you only knew what happens in the spirit when you rejoice, you would rejoice every day." When we rejoice, we are acting like sons and daughters of God! Rejoicing is an act of faith. Remember the words of Paul in Acts 27:25: "Cheer up...I believe God that it shall be as He told me." When we believe God, we can cheer up! Believing and rejoicing ushers in the glory and goodness of God in our lives.

> **IF YOU ONLY KNEW WHAT HAPPENS IN THE SPIRIT WHEN YOU REJOICE, YOU WOULD REJOICE EVERY DAY.**

> *...yet believing, ye rejoice with joy unspeakable and full of glory...*
>
> *- 1 Peter 1:8*
>
> *...even now you are happy with the inexpressible joy that comes from heaven itself.*
>
> *- Living Bible*

JOY: THE SECRET OF FAITH AND ENDURANCE

Though the fig tree does not blossom...the fields yield no food...No cattle in the stalls, Yet I will rejoice in the Lord...The Lord God is my Strength...He makes...me to walk...and make [spiritual] progress upon my high places [of trouble, suffering, or responsibility]!

- Habakkuk 3:17-19 - Amplified Bible

Rejoicing will enable us to make progress in difficult times. Joy is the secret of faith and endurance. James 1:2 says to count it all joy when trouble comes. This must be why Job laughed at destruction and trouble (Job 5:22). Of course some people may think you are a fool, but if you have found joy, you have found the secret of survival and success.

JOY'S MULTIFACETED CONNECTION

Joy is connected to: God's presence (Psalm 16:11), God's strength (Nehemiah 8:10), God's salvation (Isaiah 12:3), the anointing - the oil of joy (Hebrews 1:9), God's medicine

(Proverbs 17:22), God's Word (Jeremiah 15:16, Psalm 119:162), and prosperity (2 Corinthians 9:6 -10, Psalm 105:37 - 45). Look at all of the blessings of God that are connected to joy. It seems that if Satan can steal our joy, then he can damage a lot of other things in our lives.

JESUS STILL LAUGHS

Joy and rejoicing are simply a choice we make daily. It is clear that God did not create us to be miserable. He created us in Christ to enjoy life and to have dominion. Joy is one of the great secrets of faith. One of my favorite pictures of Jesus is the one

> JOY IS ONE OF THE GREAT SECRETS OF FAITH.

of Him laughing triumphantly. Jesus sits in the heavens and laughs (Psalm 2:4). Make the choice to rejoice!

CHAPTER TWENTY TWO: 22
MAXIMUM JOY

Consider it maximum joy, my brothers, when
you get involved in all sorts of trials...

- James 1:2 - Berkeley

In high school, I played on the championship football team. We were undefeated, so we always went out fully expecting to win. One day the coach told me, "Now Hankins," as he grabbed me by my shoulder pads, "you might be able to go around the tackle, but by the time you go around him, what you're looking for already went by." Then he said, "The only way you can play defense is to not avoid the pressure the tackle is putting on you. You can't go around him; if you do, you will miss what you're after. You've got to fight through the pressure."

The reason the devil is putting pressure on you is because God's got a blessing coming for you! So when pressure comes from every side, face it and get happy right in the middle of it! The devil is saying, "Hey, give up and just go around." You say, "No. I am not going around. I am going through this tackle!"

> *The Lord God is my strength, and he will make my feet like hinds feet, and he will make me to walk upon mine high places...*
>
> *- Habakkuk 3:19*

JOY NEUTRALIZES PRESSURE

The Apostle Paul had the Jews, the Gentiles, and the Romans putting pressure on him. During one of the most difficult hours of his life, he began singing praises to God.

> *And at midnight Paul and Silas prayed, and sang praises unto God...*
>
> *- Acts 16:25*

The devil can put pressure on you and get you into a corner, but as long as he can't shut your mouth, you are able to overcome. Oral Roberts said, "Everyday there's a miracle coming to you or passing you by." That means if you allow pressure to push you out of your position, you'll miss your miracle.

When you start counting it all joy, it neutralizes the pressure. That is a challenge, but rejoicing is a choice you make that will strengthen you so that your faith and patience will hold you steady.

...Is your life full of difficulties and temptations? Then be happy for when the way is rough, your patience has a chance to grow. So let it grow and don't try to squirm out of your problems. For when your patience is finally in full bloom, then you will be ready for anything, strong in character, full and complete.

- James 1:2-4 - Living Bible

FAITH UNDER TRIAL

I was watching a documentary on how they make pottery. Pottery is baked in extreme heat to make it durable and hard so it is usable. I thought it was interesting that they know a pot is done by the sound it makes. Many times trouble will hit you and get you into a serious oven situation. If you stay in the oven silent, then you are going to be in the oven a long time. But if you will just go ahead and shout for joy, you will make it through!

God is interested in your character, not just your immediate comfort. God wants you to hold steady and stop squirming out of your problems and difficulties prematurely. The natural human tendency is to try to find a way to get out from

> GOD IS INTERESTED IN YOUR CHARACTER AND YOUR WHOLE PERSON, NOT JUST YOUR IMMEDIATE COMFORT.

under the pressure. You have to realize that your faith is on trial and the devil is trying to knock that faith right out of you. Mix patience with your faith and it will take you through the pressure. Let God build character in you and make you strong enough to receive blessings that you may not have been able to receive before. If you will refuse to give up and allow your faith to be on trial, you cannot lose.

> *Consider it wholly joyful, my brethren, whenever you are enveloped in or encounter trials of any sort or fall into various*

118

temptations. Be assured and understand that the trial and proving of your faith bring out endurance and steadfastness and patience. But let endurance and steadfastness and patience have full play and do a thorough work so that you may be [people] perfectly and fully developed [with no defects] lacking in nothing.

- James 1:2-4 - Amplified

There hath no temptation taken you but such as is common to man: but God is faithful, who will not suffer you to be tempted above that ye are able; but will with the temptation also make a way to escape, that you may be able to bear it.

- 1 Corinthians 10:13

GOD IS RESTORING YOUR JOY

At 75 years of age, Norman Vincent Peal, was asked when were the best ten years of his life. He replied, "I haven't lived them yet!"

Shake off the dust of the past. God will restore the years that the devil tried to mess up in your life. Don't look back with regret. What the devil meant for evil, God is turning around for your good.

You have to rejoice because the new thing is going to have to come through you. God's going to do His part, but you have to do your part. God has some surprises that are exceeding abundantly above all you could ask or think according to the power that works in you (Ephesians 3:20).

23
JOY COMETH IN THE MORNING

Many are the afflictions of the righteous: but the
Lord delivereth him out of them all.

- Psalm 34:19

I'm glad that the Lord said in Psalm 34:19 that He would deliver us out of all of our afflictions. He did not say half of them or most of them, He siad, "out of them all." God always makes a way out. God always has an escape route and is faithful to bring us out. The word "afflictions" means: adversity,

> GOD ALWAYS HAS AN ESCAPE ROUTE AND IS FAITHFUL TO BRING US OUT.

distress, tribulation, persecution, depression, misery, trouble, and pressure. God never guarantees us that we will be exempt from adversity. He does guarantee to always bring us out.

...weeping may endure for a night, but joy cometh in the morning.

- Psalm 30:5

THE SUN IS COMING UP ON A NEW DAY

But unto you who revere and worshipfully fear My name shall the Sun of Righteousness arise with healing in His wings and His beams, and you shall go forth and gambol like calves [released] from the stall and leap for joy.

- Malachi 4:2 - Amplified Bible

Joy cometh in the morning. It may seem like a long night, but the night cannot last forever. The sun is coming up on a new day. The Sun of Righteousness is rising with healing in His wings (beams) and you shall go forth and grow up as calves released from the stall (Malachi 4:2). As sure as the sun comes up every morning, your deliverance is on the way.

> AS SURE AS THE SUN COMES UP EVERY MORNING, YOUR DELIVERANCE IS ON THE WAY.

is on the way. The earth is constantly turning on its axis. Even though you may not feel like it, your situation is turning right

122

now. It may seem dark now, but something is happening. Things are turning, the morning is certain, and the sun is rising. Say this out loud now: JOY COMETH!!! HEALING COMETH!!! BLESSING COMETH!!! MONEY COMETH!!! FAITH COMETH!!!

THE TURNING POINT

Thou hast turned for me my mourning into dancing: thou hast put off my sackcloth, and girded me with gladness.

- Psalm 30:11

You are at a turning point. It may seem difficult, but things are turning around for you. God is turning your depression into a celebration. It is time to change clothes. It is time to dance and rejoice. God wants to dress you up in joy. Put on your shouting clothes!

To appoint unto them that mourn in Zion, to give unto them beauty for ashes, the oil of joy for mourning, the garment of praise for the spirit of heaviness; that they might be called trees of righteousness, the planting of the Lord, that he might be glorified.

- Isaiah 61:3

123

A HAPPY APPOINTMENT

God has appointed this deliverance for you. You have a destined date with the blessing of the Lord. What seemed to be burned and ruined, God is turning into something beautiful. He is anointing you with joy. The anointing breaks every yoke, lifts every burden, and makes us laugh at the

> UNSPEAKABLE JOY IS A CONTAINER OF THE GLORY OF GOD.

enemy. Count it all joy. God has given you a garment of praise. There is great deliverance in the garment of praise. Put it on right now. Keep it on. Praise God! Praise the Lord! Thank you, Jesus! He never fails to plan the best things for us.

Unspeakable joy is a container of the glory of God. The glory and the abundance of God are manifested in an atmosphere of rejoicing. We are commanded to rejoice; it is not an option. God brought you here to have fun - now you are going to have fun! God brought you here to have victory - now you are going to have victory! Not someday in the future...NOW!!!

F or this reason I bow my knees to the Father, - the great first cause of all who claim a father, alike in Heaven and on earth. I pray that He may, with a fulness measured only by the wealth of His own glory, vouchsafe to you to be made strong with power infused by His Spirit into your inmost nature. I pray that Messiah may, through your faith, make His home in your hearts; that so, like trees, firm-rooted in love,-like temples, having a firm foundation in love – you may, in common with all His consecrated ones, be fully able to comprehend what is the breadth, the length, the depth, the height–ay, really to know the love of Messiah (which transcends all 'illumination,') that you may be filled with all the plentitude of God.

Ephesians 3:14-21

Arthur S. Way

THE
REDEMPTION
FACTOR

CHAPTER TWENTY FOUR: 24
ONCE UPON A TIME

Everyone likes a great story that begins with the phrase, "Once upon a time...." The story of Jesus is the greatest story ever told. It is not a fantasy, but a true story that has changed the world for thousands of years. The story of Jesus is told in over a thousand languages to millions of people, young and old, around the world and is still changing lives today! One day as I was studying Hebrews 9 and 10, the word "ONCE" stood out so clearly. I began to see God's plan of redemption in Christ and how the wisdom and power of God very effectively "ONCE" paid the price for our freedom.

Neither by the blood of goats and calves, but by his own blood he entered in ONCE into the holy place, having obtained eternal redemption for us.

- Hebrews 9:12

He went ONCE for all into the [Holy of] Holies... but His own blood, having found and secured a complete redemption (an everlasting release for us).

- Amplified

ONCE! That's all it took! What Jesus did for us in His death, burial, and resurrection, He only had to do ONCE! He shed His blood, ONCE! He paid the price for our freedom, ONCE! He put away and abolished sin, ONCE! He defeated and dethroned Satan, ONCE FOR ALL TIME...ONCE for all mankind...ONCE for the cure of every condition...ONCE for every blessing in Heaven to be ours!

Whenever you face any challenge, remember this story and tell it again: Once Upon a Time! When Satan comes against you, just bring up this story and say, "Once upon a time..." and he will leave. Now, we as believers can take the Word of God and tell the devil a bedtime story. Say, "Devil, ONCE upon a time Jesus defeated you for all eternity." Speak the Word of God with boldness and rock the devil to sleep!

So Christ was ONCE offered to bear the sins of many; and unto them that look for him shall he appear the second time without sin unto salvation.

- Hebrews 9:28

By the which will we are sanctified through the offering of the body of Jesus Christ ONCE for all.

- Hebrews 10:10

For by ONE offering he hath perfected for ever them that are sanctified.

- Hebrews 10:14

By looking at these scriptures we see that Jesus cancelled and abolished sin ONCE for all time and for all men. The Holy Spirit continues to emphasize the word "ONCE." We must know this story well. It is the story of Christmas, Easter, Pentecost, Heaven, and Earth. This story is well known by

THE STORY OF THE BLOOD OF JESUS IS AN ESTABLISHED FACT THROUGHOUT ETERNITY.

angels and demons. The story of the blood of Jesus is an established fact throughout eternity.

A NEW DAY OF BOLDNESS

The other word that stood out to me in Hebrews was the word, "boldness." The blood of Jesus has given us great boldness and confidence.

Having therefore, brethren, BOLDNESS to enter into the holiest by the blood of Jesus.
                                                    - Hebrews 10:19

Let us therefore come BOLDLY unto the throne of grace....

                                                    - Hebrews 4:16

...that we may BOLDLY say, The Lord is my helper....

                                                    - Hebrews 13:6

Some other translations of Hebrews 10:19 translate boldness as "freedom of speech" or "outspoken." The blood of Jesus has given us great boldness and confidence. As believers, we need to exercise our "freedom of speech" and be "outspoken" about the blood of Jesus and who we are in Christ. Instead of being a victim of our experiences, our experiences are a victim of us.

CHAPTER TWENTY FIVE: 25
THE SECRET
OF POWER...
CHRIST IN YOU

God has put us in a place where He expects us to have His latest revelation, the revelation of that marvelous fact of "Christ in us" and what this really means. The secret of power is the unveiling of Christ, the all-powerful One within, the revelation of God who comes to abide in us.

- Smith Wigglesworth

I am crucified with Christ: nevertheless I live; yet not I, but Christ lives in me and the life which I now live in the flesh I live by the faith of the Son of God, who loved me, and gave Himself for me.

- Galatians 2:20

POSITION, PRIVILEGE, POTENTIAL, POWER, PROMISE IN CHRIST

The reality of every Christian is that we are In Christ and Christ is in us. Think about these words and say them out loud, "Christ lives in me." God has placed us In Christ. This position of faith gives us great privilege. In Christ we have access to the Father with confidence and we have great potential In Him. We are ever-increasing in faith and love and are on the way to our divine destiny In Christ. The same power that raised Christ from the dead is available to believers In Christ. There are also exceeding great and precious promises that belong to us In Christ.

> THE REALITY OF EVERY CHRISTIAN IS THAT WE ARE IN CHRIST AND CHRIST IS IN US.

For all the promises of God in Him are yes and in Him amen, unto the glory of God by us.

- 2 Corinthians 1:20

In Christ, God says a giant "yes" to us and we answer "Amen, so be it!" We agree with God and live in the reality of our redemption In Christ.

135

Therefore if any man be in Christ, he is a new creature: old things are passed away; behold, all things are become new.

-2 Corinthians 5:17

For He hath made Him to be sin for us, who knew no sin; that we might be made the righteousness of God in Him.

- 2 Corinthians 5:21

In whom we have boldness and access with confidence by the faith of Him.

- Ephesians 3:12

For in Him dwelleth all the fullness of the Godhead bodily. And ye are complete in Him, which is the head of all principality and power.

- Colossians 2: 9 – 10

We enjoy great position, privilege, potential, power and promise In Christ. God sees us In Christ and we look a lot better In Christ than we do outside of Him. If you are not impressed with who you are In Christ, you haven't seen Him lately. We have come

> WE LOOK A LOT BETTER IN CHRIST THAN WE DO OUTSIDE OF HIM.

into closest fellowship with Christ. We are In Him. The Apostle Paul uses the phrase In Christ, In Him, and In Whom, over 130 times in his letters. At the cross, God was working "in" Christ but He was working "on" us. We are the workmanship of God created In Christ Jesus unto

> IF YOU ARE NOT IMPRESSED WITH WHO YOU ARE IN CHRIST, YOU HAVEN'T SEEN HIM LATELY.

good works, which God has before ordained for us to walk in them (Ephesians 2:10). Take your position In Christ and live in the privileges and advantages God has provided for you.

FINDING YOURSELF IN THE GROUP PICTURE

When looking at a group picture, the first thing you look for is yourself. The death, burial, and resurrection of Christ is a "Group Picture." You need to look for yourself in the group picture of redemption. You were included on the cross and were there in His resurrection and triumph.

The greatest of all revelations in the Bible is in Paul's New Testament letters. "Paul's letters contain the thoughts that Jesus carried away from this world unuttered. They are the advanced teachings of our Lord Jesus Christ," James Stalker. The Apostle

Paul gives us the great facts of redemption. He explains what happened in the death, burial, and resurrection of Jesus Christ. Everything Jesus did, He did for us and has set it to the credit of our account as though we did it. We were identified with Him.

Many years ago, Dad Hagin instructed us to go through Paul's letters in the New Testament and underline every time we saw the phrases In Christ, In Him, and In Whom. He said to write those scriptures down and daily meditate on them. He also said to confess "this is who I am and this is what I have In Christ." E.W. Kenyon said, "Many Christians are weak, though they are sincere because they have never dared to make a bold confession of who they are In Christ."

> **AT THE CROSS GOD WAS WORKING "IN" CHRIST, BUT HE WAS WORKING "ON" US.**

> *And hath raised us up together and made us sit together in heavenly places in Christ Jesus.*
>
> *- Ephesians 2:6*

We were crucified with Christ, made alive with Him, and raised up together with Him. We are now seated together with Him and blessed with every spiritual blessing in heavenly places in Christ.

CHAPTER
TWENTY SIX:
26
JESUS IN
YOUR JERSEY

He that spared not his own Son, but delivered him up for us all, how shall he not with him also freely give us all things?

- Romans 8:32

How, then, shall we respond to all this? If God is rootin' for us, who can win over us? If he didn't hold back his own Son, but put him in the game for us all, won't he even more gladly, in addition to his Son, equip us with all we need to win the game?

- Jordan

I played football in high school so I know what it means to come in as a substitute for somebody. If you have ever watched a football game on TV, you hear announcers giving their commentary on what is taking place in the game. You may hear the announcer talk about a particular player, let's say number 65 (that was my number in high school). The guys on the other team are pounding him all over the field and stomping him really bad. He is bleeding and has grass stains and dirt all over him. Every time the ball is hiked, number 65 gets slaughtered. He gets pushed so far back that you think he's on the other team. Number 65 is just being dominated by the other team. Then the coach says, "I've got a plan." He pulls number 65 out and replaces him with the strongest man on the team.

GOD'S GOT A PLAN

That's what God did for us when He sent Jesus to die in our place. God put Jesus in number 65's (mankind's) jersey. Number 65 runs back on the field, and now the whole picture changes. The announcer says, "You know, something has happened to number 65. He's moving that ball all over the field now."

Before man was identified with Christ in His death, burial, and resurrection, he had been whipped all over by depression, discouragement, fear, failure, shame, and guilt. But now, number 65 is winning and he's dominating.

God saw our condition and knew that He could not train us enough to change the game. He knew there was no other way than to get in our jersey. He said, "We can't train them, let's just jump on the inside of them. I'll live on the inside of them. I'll walk in them." God moved on the inside of you and got in your jersey. He identified with you so you could identify with Him.

I am crucified with Christ: nevertheless I live; yet not I, but Christ liveth in me: and the life which I now live in the flesh I live by the faith of the Son of God, who loved me, and gave himself for me.

- Galatians 2:20

"Identification" is defined in Webster's Dictionary as: "to consider or treat as the same, the condition or fact of being, the same in all qualities under consideration." These words are all related to each other: identification, identity, identical, and identified. Many people live and die and never really find their true identity.

PROOF OF IDENTIFICATION

Have you ever checked in for a flight and been asked for proof of identification? You can say, "Here I am. Can't you see - this is me? I can prove that I exist. Just look." Even when I played baseball in elementary school, they wanted to see my birth certificate! I could have said, "Look, I can prove I was born. Here I am." That was not enough. I needed some authentic, legal, official proof that I was who I said I was. This is all a part of life in this natural world.

In the realm of the Spirit you say, "Well, here I am. Obviously, I am who I am." God will ask, "Do you have any identification on you?" You say, "I sure do, I have some identification right here in Galatians 2:20: I am crucified with Christ: nevertheless I live; yet not I but Christ liveth in me."

CHAPTER TWENTY SEVEN: 27
ENGRAFTED INTO CHRIST

The two words "In Christ" are the most important words used by the Apostle Paul in the New Testament. AJ Gordon said it this way, "These two words 'In Christ' give us profound insight into the Divine method of salvation. These two words open to us mysteries and secrets that were hidden for ages and generations." These words are the key to opening the secrets of the Gospel. We have been "In Christed." There are over130 scriptures that use the phrase In Christ, In Him, and In Whom. What do these phrases mean?

> *Therefore if any person is [ENGRAFTED] in Christ (the Messiah) he is a new creation (a new creature altogether); the old [previous moral and spiritual condition] has passed away. Behold the fresh and new has come!*
>
> *- 2 Corinthians 5:17 - Amplified*

We have been engrafted into Christ. He is the vine and we are the branches.

I live in an area where there are a lot of plant nurseries. These nurseries have millions and millions of plants that are shipped all over the United States. One thing I have learned from the nurseries is the engrafting process.

Graft – to insert (a shoot from one plant) into another living plant so that the two grow together as a single plant.

The stock of the plant must be cut with the same identical wound as the branch in order for the two to grow together. Then, you must put that branch inside of the open wound of the plant and wrap them together and they will become one. On the cross, Jesus was wounded with our identical condition and we were placed In Him. There is no "grafting" without wounding.

Surely he hath borne our griefs, and carried our sorrows: yet we did esteem him stricken, smitten of God, and afflicted. But he was WOUNDED for our transgressions, he was bruised for our iniquities: the chastisement of our peace was upon him; and with his stripes we are healed.

- Isaiah 53:4-5

Jesus took our guilt, shame, sin, death, and curse so that we could be free. We were engrafted into His death that we might be one with His resurrection and victory. He was made to be sin for us that we might be made the righteousness of God In Him (2 Corinthians 5:21).

We are new creatures In Christ and God would not make an unrighteous new creature. We have the same righteousness as Jesus Christ Himself. He took our shame that we may live without guilt. We can now face life confident that we are qualified for God's best blessings.

For the scripture saith, Whosoever believeth on him shall not be ashamed.

- Romans 10:11

In the body of his flesh through death, to present you holy and unblameable and unreproveable in his sight.

- Colossians 1:22

SHAME-FREE LIVING

Shame is the issue that drives almost every compulsive, self-defeating behavior known to the human race. Shame is at the root of all addictions. It may be forgotten, hidden, or disguised, but the shame is there, is real, and it drives behavior. Sometimes the shame surfaces first. In other cases, the addiction surfaces first. Whenever we encounter one, we always look for the other. Shame and addiction can always be found together.

- The Complete Life Encyclopedia

It is especially interesting that professional psychiatrists recognize the power and influence of shame in shaping people today. It drives human behavior. Many have misdiagnosed their own problems and conditions. This has caused many to try to fix their behavior with more and more doses of shame and guilt. Instead of curing the problem, shame perpetuates the problem. The cure is at the cross of Jesus Christ. On the cross, God was working in Christ but He was working on us. Jesus took our condition and we were engrafted into Him. Now, God sees us In Christ. We must consistently see ourselves in the light of the death, burial, and resurrection. We look a lot better In Christ than we do outside of Him. He sees us through the blood, through the cross, and through the resurrection. He has raised us up together with Christ and seated us together with Him. We reign in life through the abundance of grace and the gift of righteousness through one man Jesus Christ (Romans 5:17).

RIGHTEOUSNESS:
REVELATION AND MOTIVATION

It is important to understand that the Gospel of Christ is a revelation of righteousness (Romans 1:16–17). Understanding righteousness is fundamental to Christianity. Understanding righteousness also enables us to win the fight of faith. The Apostle Paul's letters help us to understand that righteousness is a free gift. His letters also help us to see ourselves "In Christ."

Righteousness gives us right standing with God. Righteousness sets us free from a sense of sin, guilt, and shame. Since we are free from the motivating power of shame, we are now under a new motivating power of righteousness. The power of righteousness is the revelation of all true victory. We are no longer haunted by a sense of inadequacy or inferiority. God has given us "first-class" righteousness In Christ!

LET THE
GOOD
TIMES
ROLL

CHAPTER TWENTY EIGHT: 28
GOD IS A REWARDER

The Lord recompense thy work, and a full reward be given thee of the Lord God of Israel, under whose wings thou art come to trust.

- Ruth 2:12

May the Lord reward your kindness...

- Berkeley

God is a rewarder! God told Abraham, "Fear not...I am your shield and exceeding great reward," (Genesis 15:1). Think of the great rewards that God gave to Abraham and his descendants because he believed and obeyed God. Abraham, the father of faith, knew God as a rewarder.

The word "recompense" simply means "payday". God has a definite payday for your work of faith. My Dad, B.B.

Hankins, always said, "With God, payday is not always on Friday, but God's paydays always come."

A full and exceeding great reward be given you of the Lord! God has a great payday of blessing for you. Everyone is happier on payday. You can rejoice because there is a payday on the way!

> **WITH GOD, PAYDAY IS NOT ALWAYS ON FRIDAY, BUT GOD'S PAYDAYS ALWAYS COME.**

GIVING ACCESSES THE GLORY

But my God shall supply all your need according to his riches in glory by Christ Jesus.

- Philippians 4:19

Paul said to the Philippian believers, "because you gave, and gave again, I have all and abound." Philippians 4:19 was given to people who were partners with Paul. Their giving tapped into God's riches in glory.

You can see the same principle with Cornelius in Acts 10. He was a devout man that feared God. He gave "much alms to the people, and prayed to God always," Acts 10:2. His prayers and his giving came up as a memorial before God and the glory of God came to his family. Cornelius and his whole house were filled with the Holy Spirit. Some of God's paydays are better than money!

A GREAT PAYDAY...ON THE WAY

Years ago, Trina and I were believing God for a financial breakthrough. We had been faithfully giving over 30 percent of our income and were believing that God would multiply our seed sown. One night, I dreamed I ate a Payday candy bar. So the next morning, I went to the local store, bought me a Payday candy bar, and ate it. I told Trina, "It's payday." Within 24 hours, we had a pressed down, shaken together, and running over harvest come in! There is a payday! God is a rewarder!

DOUBLE PAYDAY

Instead of your [former] shame you shall have a twofold recompense; instead of dishonor and reproach [your people] shall rejoice in their portion. Therefore in their land they shall

possess double [what they had forfeited];
everlasting joy shall be theirs.

- Isaiah 61:7, Amplified Bible

For years, Trina and I had been sowing seed and believing God for a plane for the ministry. We had found a Cessna 421 and were making arrangements to purchase it. The next week at our annual leadership conference, we were blessed with over half of the money needed to purchase the plane. We were so thankful for the Lord's abundant provision and were continuing to believe God for the plane to be completely paid for.

The following weekend, we went to Dallas for my nephew's wedding. When we checked into our hotel, a mistake had been made in the reservations. Instead of a room with a king-size bed, I was given a room with two double beds. We were frustrated and were planning on changing the arrangements. My kids even offered to give us their room because they had a king-size bed.

When I turned and looked at the bed, I saw a Payday candy bar on the pillow. Then I realized that there was a Payday candy bar on each bed. When I saw that, I told my kids, "You go ahead and go to your room. We will stay right here." Trina and I opened our Payday candy bars, ate them and rejoiced saying, "It must be a double payday!" The following Sunday, someone came to our church and gave an offering that completely paid off the plane! **OUR DOUBLE PAYDAY HAD COME!!!**

> *Turn you to the stronghold, ye prisoners of hope: even today do I delcare that I will render double unto thee.*
>
> *- Zechariah 9:12*

> *Return to the stronghold [of security and prosperity], you prisoners of hope; even today do I declare that I will restore double your former prosperity to you.*
>
> *- Amplified*

Your payday is coming! Sow a double seed and do a double dance. Get filled with the Holy Ghost. For your double trouble, God will give you a double measure of joy, wealth, and anointing. Just like Job, God is going to give you twice as much as you had before!

CHAPTER TWENTY NINE: 29
HEAVEN ON EARTH

We are living in days of great glory, when the glory and the goodness of God break into our lives on a scale that is unprecedented. Whenever we say "glory" we are including all of the goodness of God. One commentary defined the glory this way: wealth, numbers, commerce, power, wisdom, promotion, superiority, dignity, authority, nobility, splendor, valor, magnificence, extraordinary privileges and advantages. Jesus came to restore the glory that God intended for us to have! This is the time of the restoration of glory in the church around the world!

> *But as truly as I live, all the earth shall be filled with the glory of the Lord.*
>
> *- Numbers 14:21*

For the earth shall be filled with the knowledge of the glory of the Lord, as the waters cover the sea.

- Habakkuk 2:14

In Deuteronomy 11:21, the phrase "as the days of heaven upon the earth" is used to describe the special time of blessing the children of God would enjoy in the Promised Land. God gave them instructions on how to act to possess the land. He actually uses the word "possess" seven times in this chapter. Over and over He tells them they must possess this land of promise.

NEVER LOOK BACK

We know that God is a faith God and He is pleased by faith. I like to say "faith cranks God's tractor." It is necessary for us to believe God to enter into all that He has provided for us. We must maintain a spirit of faith to go forward in this time. According to Philippians 3:12-14, we press forward and never look back. Smith Wigglesworth said, "Never look back if you want the power of God in your life."

EXPERIENCE THE GLORY

In 1906, one of the greatest outpourings of the Holy Spirit occurred in California at Azusa Street. From this outpouring, revivals were sparked all over the world. It is time for us to experience the glory of God in our generation.

> *But we all, with open face beholding as in a glass the glory of the Lord, are changed into the same image from glory to glory, even as by the Spirit of the Lord.*
>
> *- 2 Corinthians 3:18*

> *...ever increasing splendor and from one degree of glory to another...*
>
> *- Amplified*

God is called the "God of Glory" in Acts 7:2. In Ephesians 1:17, God is the "Father of Glory." In Psalm 24:7-10, He is the "King of Glory." In 1 Corinthians 2:8, Jesus is called the "Lord of Glory." In Hebrews 2:10, we see that Jesus died to bring "many sons unto glory." 2 Corinthians 3:18 says that we are changed from "glory to glory." 1 Peter 4:14 says, "...the Spirit of glory and of God resteth upon you...." In 1 Corinthians 2:7, the Apostle Paul says of his revelation, "But we speak the wisdom of God in a mystery, even the hidden wisdom, which God ordained before the world unto our glory." Jesus came that we might enjoy the same glory (John 17:22-24).

KEEP YOUR CONFIDENCE

Cast not away therefore your confidence, which hath great recompense of reward.

- Hebrews 10:35

Knowing that whatsoever good thing any man doeth, the same shall he receive of the Lord...

- Ephesians 6:8

Keep your confidence. There is a great payday that is certain. Hebrew 10:36 says, "For you have need of patience...." Keep believing and obeying God and His Word. Your payday is on the way. God is a rewarder. We have great confidence and expectation in the Lord. God's reward system is unlimited!

He is the Almighty God, the Father of the whole family in Heaven and Earth. He is the God and Father of our Lord Jesus Christ, the Father of Glory. Ephesians 3:20 says, "Now unto Him that is able to do exceeding abundantly above all we ask or think, according to the power that worketh in us." The days of Heaven on Earth have already begun and they will multiply. We will see the goodness and glory of God.

CONTEND FOR THE GLORY

Now is the time for us to contend for the glory. The glory of God will increase for those who believe. The glory of the Lord is God's manifested presence. In His presence is fullness of joy so there must be some extraordinary joy in the glory (1 Peter 1:8). Unspeakable joy is a container of the glory of God.

The first thing we should do is believe and declare it. Expect it and it shall come to pass! We are living in the last days. The promises and prophesies are being fulfilled faster and faster. The atmosphere of Heaven and the aroma of praise are filling the church. Be strengthened in your faith and position yourself for "Heaven on Earth!"

Jesus said if you will believe, you will see the glory of God (John 11:40). Jesus was not talking about some day far into the future - He was speaking of a manifestation of God's goodness and power, now! This is the day the Lord has made, let us rejoice and be glad in it! Go ahead and rejoice like your dream is coming to pass! **LET THE GOOD TIMES ROLL!!!**

Mark and Trina Hankins travel nationally and internationally preaching the Word of God with the power of the Holy Spirit. Their message centers on the spirit of faith... who the believer is in Christ...and the work of the Holy Spirit with joy.

Mark Hankins' daily radio program, "Taking Your Place In Christ," is heard across the United States. It is also made available internationally, via the internet at www.markhankins.org. He is the author of nine books: *Let the Good Times Roll, Revolutionary Revelation, The Spirit of Faith, Taking Your Place In Christ, The Power of Identification with Christ, Spirit-Filled Study Guide, Never Run At Your Giant With Your Mouth Shut, Acknowledging Every Good Thing That Is In You In Christ,* and *11:23-The Language of Faith.*

Trina is an anointed praise and worship leader and recording artist. She has recorded two albums: A Place By the Father and Be It Unto Me.

Mark and Trina Hankins are also the pastors of Christian Worship Center in Alexandria, Louisiana. Their son, Aaron Hankins and his wife, Errin Cody, serve as associate pastors of Christian Worship Center. Their daughter, Alicia Moran and her husband, Caleb, serve as directors of Mark Hankins Ministries.

The Snow Kids Song

If you wanna have fun in the snow
Im gonna tell you all what you need
to know
All the snow kids at snowman school
Know that snow is cold but I am cool

Its cold cold cold dude
But Im cool cool cool
Watch Me Now

When Im goin down hill I go real fast
Everybody waves as I zoom past
All the snow kids know the #1 rule
That snow is cold but I stay cool

Goin down the slopes I always zoom
I tell everyone to gimme some Room
The snow kids know their snow kid rules
Its that snow is cold but I am cool.

When my toes get cold & We had enough
I dont quit when the going get tough
The snow kids shout......

ACKNOWLEDGMENTS

Special Thanks To

My wife, Trina

My son, Aaron and his wife, Errin Cody

their daughters, Avery Jane and Macy Claire.

My daughter, Alicia and her husband, Caleb

their son, Jaiden Mark.

Mark Hankins Ministries Staff for research,

editing and project design.

REFERENCES

Amplified Bible. Zondervan Publishing House, Grand Rapids, Michigan, 1972.

Barclay, William. *New Testament Words.* The Westminster Press, Philadelphia, Pennsylvania, 1964.

Frankl, Viktor. *Man's Search for Meaning.* Washington Square Press, New York, New York, 1984.

Gordon, A.J. *The Ministry of the Spirit.* Lamplighter Publications, Alexandria, Louisiana.

Gordon, A.J. *In Christ.* Wade Pickren Publications, Revised 1983.

Kenyon, E.W. *The Two Kinds of Life.* Kenyon's Publishing Society, 1997.

Knox, Ronald. *The Old Testament Newly Translated from the Latin Vulgate.* Burns, Oates and Washbourne, Ltd., London, England, 1949.

Maxwell, John. *Be a People Person.* Victor Books, a division of Scripture Press Publication Inc, US, Canada, England, 1989.

Minirth, Frank, Paul Meier, and Stephen Arterburn. *The Complete Life Encyclopedia.* Thomas Nelson Publishers, Nashville, Tennessee, 1995.

Morgan, Louis. "Azusa Street Centential," *History of the Azusa Street Revival*, http://www.azusastreet100.net/history.htm (accessed May 10, 2006).

Nelson, P.C. *Bible Doctrines.* Gospel Publishing House,

Springfield, Missouri, 1971.

New American Bible. Thomas Nelson Publishers, New York, New York, 1975.

Peterson, Eugene. *The Message/Remix, The Bible in Contemporary Language.* NavPress Publishing Group, Colorado Springs, Colorado, 2003.

Phillips, J.B. *The New Testament in Modern English.* The Macmillan Company, New York, New York, 1959.

Rotherham, J.B. *The Emphasized Bible.* Kregel Publications, Grand Rapids, Michigan, 1976.

Stalker, James. *The Life of St. Paul.* Zondervan Corporation. Grand Rapids Michigan, 1983.

Sumrall, Lester. *Pioneers of Faith.* Harrison House, Tulsa, Oklahoma, 1995.

Taylor, Ken. *The Living Bible.* Tyndale House Publishers, Wheaton, Illinios, 1971.

Verkuyl, Gerrit. *The Holy Bible, The New Berkeley Version Revised Edition, in Modern English.* Zondervan Publishing House, Grand Rapids, Michigan, 1969.

Way, Arthur S. *The Letter of St. Paul to the Seven Churches and Three Friends with the Letters to the Hebrews, Sixth Edition.* Macmillian and Company, New York, New York, 1926.

Webster's II New College Dictionary. Houghton Mifflin Company, Boston, Massachusets, 1995.

Webster, Noah. *The American Dictionary of the English Language, 1828.* *www.cbtministries.org/resources/webster1828.htm*

Wigglesworth, Smith. *Ever Increasing Faith.* Gospel Publishing House, Springfield, Missouri, 1996.

Mark Hankins Ministries Publications

SPIRIT-FILLED SCRIPTURE STUDY GUIDE
A comprehensive study of scriptures in over 120 different translations on topics such as: Redemption, Faith, Finances, Prayer and many more!

THE POWER OF IDENTIFICATION WITH CHRIST
This book focuses on the reality of redemption and your new identity in Christ. As a new creature, you have everything you need inside of you to succeed in life!

THE SPIRIT OF FAITH
If you only knew what was on the other side of your mountain, you would move it! Having a spirit of faith is necessary to do the will of God and fulfill your destiny.

NEVER RUN AT YOUR GIANT
WITH YOUR MOUTH SHUT
When David ran at Goliath, there was a war of words going on. In this book, we learn that winning the war of words is necessary to winning the fight of faith.

11:23 - THE LANGUAGE OF FAITH
Never underestimate the power of one voice! Over 100 inspirational, mountain-moving quotes to "stir up" the spirit of faith in you.

TAKING YOUR PLACE IN CHRIST
Many Christians talk about what they are trying to be and what they are going to be. This book is about who you are NOW as a believer in Christ.

**ACKNOWLEDGING EVERY GOOD THING
THAT IS IN YOU IN CHRIST**
This mini-book encourages every believer to have a daily
confession or acknowledgment of who they are in Christ.

REVOLUTIONARY REVELATION
This book provides excellent insight on how the spirit of
wisdom and revelation is mandatory for believers to access
their call, inheritance, and authority in Christ.

Purchasing and Contact Information:

MARK HANKINS MINISTRIES
PO BOX 12863
ALEXANDRIA, LA 71315

Phone: 318.448.4500
Fax: 318.443.2948

E-mail: contact@markhankins.org

Visit us on the web:
www.markhankins.org